Praise for
The 5 Languages of Appreciation in the Workplace

This is not just a "good book," it is a great tool—a well thought through, well researched, and thoughtfully applied resource to empower your people, increase unity and productivity, and reduce turnover. The moment I finished I wanted to do a staff retreat and get this in the hands of our HR department. I highly recommend it.

> **—Chip Ingram**
> Author of *Holy Ambition*
> President and Teaching Pastor of Living on the Edge

If the insights and wisdom offered by Chapman and White are practiced in the workplace, churches, and voluntary organizations, there will be a glorious revolution in human relations.

> **—Lyle W. Dorsett**
> Billy Graham Professor of Evangelism
> Beeson Divinity School
> Samford University

Personal dignity and self-respect have always been hallmarks of the values needed to sustain relationships in business and in life. I love what Gary and Paul have created, and, as with all things great, it's exactly what we need based on this time in our nation's history and the pressures our businesses and families are under.

Our businesses are really organisms—not mechanisms—that require care and feeding. This book will feed the individuals who really value how we treat people and who want to stretch their commitment to doing the right thing, not just for their business but also for the employees and communities they serve.

> **—Peter Strople,** CEO
> Zero2 Holdings
> Former Dell executive

I had no idea! There are five different languages of appreciation, and we don't all speak the same language? As I read the book and thought about it, it made total sense to me. Motivational management skills are critical to my team's long-term success. After reading *The 5 Languages of Appreciation in the Workplace* I am now better equipped to inspire top performance in my staff by applying a very thoughtful, simple, and personalized methodology to showing my true appreciation for quality work.

> **—Jane Corwin**
> Senior Associate Director
> Princeton University—Office of Gift Planning

The insights in this book are invaluable whether you are an employer, employee, or volunteer. The principles the authors describe nurture a healthy, enjoyable, motivating environment. I'm already telling my friends, "Get this book!"

—**Norm Wakefield**
Professor Emeritus
Phoenix Seminary

To empower an organization, you have to empower its people. To empower people, leaders have to demonstrate appreciation in ways that maximize the impact for each individual. In *The 5 Languages of Appreciation in the Workplace*, Drs. Chapman and White teach us concepts that have the potential to change the work environment and culture of organizations around the world. A must read for every relationship manager.

—**George W. Hester**
Chairman/CEO
Navitas, Ltd.

Every management course highlights the value of appreciation, but appreciating me in a way that I can't hear feels very much like not being appreciated. Just as *The 5 Love Languages* enables couples to feel loved in a way that they understand, so do *The 5 Languages of Appreciation* ensure that staff know they are appreciated. This book is an important contribution to making the workplace a more pleasant environment where people feel appreciated—a prerequisite for being more productive.

—**Ian Mann**
Gateways Business Consultants Director

In far too many workplaces results matter more than the people who work there. Gary Chapman and Paul White beg to differ. In this absolute must-read book they shift the pendulum to the art of appreciation. In creative, yet very practical ways they show how to appreciate every single person at work, which will automatically boost the employee's confidence and productivity. This book holds the key to transforming all working environments into safe and effective spaces where people can feel valued once again.

—**Stephan Joubert**
International leadership consultant and
author of more than forty books

I am glad that Dr. Gary Chapman and Dr. Paul White have written this timely book. I don't know a more dignified and effective workforce than one operating from a position of worth, integrity, and confidence, as well as one that excels in language of appreciation. This book will help you transform the workplace with godly values and a simple "People Come First!" approach.

—**Tan Sri Francis Yeoh**, CBE
Managing Director, YTL Group of Companies
Primus Inter Pares (First Among Equals)
Honoree of the 2010 Oslo Business for Peace Award

The 5 Languages
of
Appreciation
in the Workplace

Empowering Organizations
by Encouraging People

GARY D. CHAPMAN
PAUL E. WHITE

NORTHFIELD PUBLISHING

CHICAGO

Edited by Elizabeth Cody Newenhuyse
Cover design: John Hamilton Design
Interior design: Smartt Guys design
5 Languages of Appreciation icon series copyright © 2010 by Dr. Paul White and TriLion Studios. All rights reserved.
Chapman Photo Credit: Boyce Shore and Associates

Library of Congress Cataloging-in-Publication Data
Chapman, Gary D.
The 5 languages of appreciation in the workplace : empowering organizations by encouraging people / Gary D. Chapman and Paul E. White.
    p. cm.
Includes bibliographical references.
Hardback ISBN 978-0-8024-6198-8   International ISBN 978-0-8024-6199-5
1. Employee motivation. 2. Personnel management. I. White, Paul E.,
II. Title. III. Title: Five languages of appreciation in the
workplace.
HF5549.5.M63C438 2011
658.3'14--dc22

2011004614

Also available as an EBook 978-0-8024-7792-8

We hope you enjoy this book from Northfield Publishing. Our goal is to provide high-quality, thought-provoking books and products that connect truth to your real needs and challenges. For more information on other books and products written and produced from a truth perspective, go to www.moodypublishers.com or write to:

Northfield Publishing
820 N. LaSalle Boulevard
Chicago, IL 60610

This book is printed on acid free recycled paper containing 30% PCW (Post Consumer Waste) and manufactured in the United States of America by R R Donnelley.

1 3 5 7 9 10 8 6 4 2

Printed in the United States of America

Contents

Preface

When I wrote the book *The Five Love Languages: The Secret to Love That Lasts*, I had no idea that the book would sell six million copies in English and be translated into forty languages around the world. However, I did know that the concept of the five love languages had the potential of greatly enhancing marital relationships. Early in my counseling career, I learned that what makes one person feel loved does not necessarily make another person feel loved. I discovered that many couples were sincerely expressing love but were not connecting emotionally because they were failing to speak each other's primary love language.

As I lead marriage seminars across the country, every week couples say to me, "We were contemplating divorce. When someone gave us a copy of your book, it literally saved our marriage." The emotional need for love is foundational to marital happiness. When that need is not met, the marital relationship tends to grow cold. On the other hand, when couples feel loved the marital relationship is positive and influences all the rest of life.

Over the last fifteen years, numerous individuals have shared with me how they have applied the concept of *The Five Love Languages* in their vocational settings. One supervisor said, "We don't call them love languages. We call them appreciation languages. But it is the same concept and it really is powerful. It has greatly enhanced the work climate in our office. Our employees are happier and more productive."

Many people have encouraged me to write a book on the languages of appreciation and the impact they can have on employee satisfaction and increased productivity. Since my experience has been in the area of marriage and family counseling, I wanted to find a coauthor who had both the academic credentials and business experience. When I met Dr. Paul White, I knew that I had found such a person. For the past several years, Dr. White has specialized in helping family-owned businesses effectively pass the company to the next generation. In that role, he has interfaced intimately with numerous leaders in various types of organizations.

For the past three years, Dr. White and I have been working together on the *Motivating by Appreciation Project*. We began by creating the **MBA Inventory**, which helps individual employees discover their primary appreciation language, their secondary language, and the language that is least meaningful to them. Using this inventory, Dr. White has conducted pilot projects in various business settings. The feedback has been extremely encouraging. We have discovered that, indeed, what makes one employee feel appreciated is not what makes another employee feel appreciated. However, when a supervisor or fellow employee learns to speak the primary appreciation language of the individual, the results are truly significant. Therefore, it is with a great deal of excitement that we launch this book, *The 5 Languages of*

Appreciation in the Workplace. It is our desire that the book and the **MBA Inventory** will be used to help thousands of business leaders create a more positive work climate and enhance the productivity of their employees by learning to speak their primary language of appreciation.

We sincerely believe that what you are about to read will enable you to create a corporate climate where individuals feel deeply appreciated—individuals who will respond to that appreciation with renewed loyalty and strengthened commitment to the success of the company.

GARY D. CHAPMAN, PHD

Introduction

Do you feel appreciated by the people with whom you work? If so, then you probably enjoy going to work each day. However, if you do not feel appreciated, then your work may simply be a means of keeping food on the table. All of us expect to get paid for the work we do unless we are a volunteer. Most paid employees would like to make more money. But the number one factor in job satisfaction is not the amount of pay but whether or not the individual feels appreciated and valued for the work they do. According to research conducted by the US Department of Labor, 64 percent of Americans who leave their jobs say they do so because they don't feel appreciated.[1] This is true of employees across the board, from CEOs to housekeeping staff. Something deep within the human psyche cries out for appreciation. When that need is unmet, then job satisfaction will be diminished.

*The number one factor in job satisfaction is not the amount of pay but **whether or not the individual feels appreciated and valued** for the work they do.*

Here are the comments of three employees who work in very different settings—but share a desire to feel appreciated.

"I would not be leaving if I just knew that they valued the work I do," Dave said. Dave was a thirty-year-old assistant to the CFO of a commercial real estate firm. He had been working for the firm for about fifteen months and initially was excited about the opportunity the position gave him for personal and professional growth. But over time, he grew more and more disillusioned.

Dave informed us he had resigned from his current accounting position and was moving to a different firm. "It's not about money. It's just that, no matter what I do—how long I work or what I accomplish—I never hear anything positive. If I make a mistake, I hear about it immediately, but if I do my job well, there is silence."

* * * * *

In a session we were conducting with the staff of a successful manufacturing company, Cindy chortled, "That will be the day!"

"What?" one of the other staff asked her.

We had just given each of the staff the results from their **Motivating by Appreciation (MBA) Inventory**, and they were reading through the report before we discussed the results as a group. Cindy's results showed that her primary language of appreciation is *acts of service.* Cindy is the type of person who is encouraged when coworkers pitch in and help her get tasks done, especially when the workload is exceptionally heavy.

Cindy happened to be the executive assistant to the patriarch and CEO of a family-owned business. She had worked for him for over twenty years, and knew him as well as anyone. Even though Mr. Stevens, who was now in his seventies, only worked part-time, Cindy still had plenty of work to do—planning his extensive travel, managing his personal affairs, and keeping him up-to-date on how the business was doing.

Cindy stated in her MBA report that if her colleagues (or supervisor) wanted to show their appreciation for her, they could help her get her work done if she was feeling overwhelmed. She said, "If Mr. Stevens lifted one finger to help me get something done, I'd fall over and die from a heart attack." She was joking—but there was an edge to the humor.

We knew, as did her colleagues, that Cindy had decided to "bide her time." She earned good money (she reportedly was the highest-paid executive assistant in the community) and was close to retirement age. And even though she was one of the most dissatisfied and one of the angriest employees, she probably wasn't going to quit anytime soon—much to the chagrin of her colleagues.

* * * * *

"I love working here!" Tammy exclaimed. "I can't think of any other place I would rather work than for Dr. Jones," she continued, sharing her thoughts with a smile. "Now, don't get me wrong. Dr. Jones is demanding. He expects you to do your work well. We work hard, see a lot of patients, and we are all held accountable for getting our tasks completed with the highest level of quality care for our patients."

We had heard from other sources that Dr. Jones, an optometrist, worked hard, efficiently, and provided excellent care for his patients. And we had heard that medical assistants were lined

"You couldn't get me to go work for any other office, no matter how much you paid me."

up waiting to work for him.

"Why do you enjoy working here so much?" I (Paul) inquired.

"Because he treats us so well. Although the work is intense and fast-paced, he is always doing things to make sure that we feel cared for."

I was intrigued by her statement of feeling cared for. "Really? Like what? How does he communicate a sense of caring to you and the rest of the staff?"

"Well, first, we have a weekly staff meeting at which we discuss what is going on in the office—what is working well, and areas that are creating challenges for us. And we discuss how to make things go better.

"Once a month he orders in lunch for the staff (we take an extra half hour for these lunches). Sometimes he will share new research or new techniques in the field with us during this time. And at Christmastime he gives us a paid day to go shopping and gives us a hundred-dollar gift card to use at the mall. But most of all, he is positive and encouraging to us. He frequently tells us that we are doing a good job—both individually, and as a team.

"You couldn't get me to go work for any other office, no matter how much you paid me."

* * * * *

THE FIVE LOVE LANGUAGES **GOES TO WORK**

Here are three real-life examples of the impact of feeling appreciated or unappreciated in the workplace. These sentiments are repeated over and over, thousands of times, in a variety of work settings. The reality is that what makes one person feel appreciated does not make another person feel appreciated. Thus, even in companies where recognition is deemed important, efforts at expressing appreciation are often ineffective.

As a result of the significant impact *The Five Love Languages* has had on millions of personal relationships and the critical importance that effective communication of appreciation and encouragement has in the workplace, we have pursued applying these concepts to work-based relationships. The goals of this book are:

> *The reality is that **what makes one person feel appreciated** does not make another person feel appreciated.*

- to inform you about the concept of languages of appreciation, practically describing what they are and what they look like in daily life;

- to help you identify your primary, secondary, and least meaningful languages of appreciation (by using the **Motivating by Appreciation Inventory**);

- to assist you in seeing how the languages of appreciation can be utilized to improve workplace relationships in a variety of contexts;

- to give you tools and suggestions for applying the principles in your daily life.

Let's get started by first understanding the concept of appreciation in the workplace and its importance for developing and maintaining positive work-based relationships.

Foundations

The Concept

I (Gary) was having dinner with a friend who is a paid employee of a large nonprofit organization. I shared with him that Dr. White and I were working on the *Motivating by Appreciation Project*. When I finished my brief overview, I said to him, "Could I ask you a personal question about your own work?" "Certainly," he said.

I continued, "On a scale of 0–10, how appreciated do you feel by your immediate supervisor?" "About 5," he said. I could detect a tinge of disappointment in his voice when he said 5.

My second question followed. "On a scale of 0–10, how appreciated do you feel by your coworkers?" "About an 8," he said. "How many people work closely with you?" I inquired. "Two," he responded. "Do you feel equally appreciated by the two of them?" I asked. "No," he said. "One would be a 6 and the other a 9. That's why I said about an 8."

Research indicates that employees favor recognition from managers and supervisors by a margin of 2–1 over recognition from coworkers.[1] However, most of us would agree that if we feel appreciated by our coworkers, life is much more pleasant. Whether you are a business owner, CEO, supervisor, or a coworker, this book is designed to help you communicate appreciation in a way that will be meaningful to the individuals with whom you work.

> *Each of us wants to know that **what we are doing matters.***

Why is feeling appreciated so important in a work setting? Because each of us wants to know that what we are doing matters. Without a sense of being valued by supervisors and colleagues, workers start to feel like a machine or a commodity. If no one notices a person's commitment to doing the job well, motivation tends to diminish over time. Steven Covey, author of the bestselling *The 7 Habits of Highly Effective People*, feels so strongly about people's need for appreciation that he states: "Next to physical survival, the greatest need of a human being is psychological survival, to be understood, to be affirmed, to be validated, to be appreciated."[2]

When relationships are *not* nurtured by a sense of appreciation, the results are predictable:

- Team members will experience a lack of connectedness with others and with the mission of the organization.

- Workers will tend to become discouraged, feeling "There is always more to do and no one appreciates what I'm doing."

- Often employees will begin to complain about their work, their colleagues, and their supervisor.

• Eventually, team members start to think seriously about leaving the organization and they begin to search for other employment.

WHY "JUST SAY THANKS" DOESN'T WORK

Communicating appreciation to employees and colleagues sounds pretty easy and straightforward. In many ways, it is. However, we also know that for the communication of appreciation to effectively encourage the other person, several factors must be considered.

First, researchers have found that attempts to communicate appreciation globally across an organization are not very effective. *For recognition and appreciation to be effective, they must be individualized and delivered personally.* Trying a general "just say thanks" campaign across the company will not have much impact. In fact, in our work with companies, we have found that this type of approach can actually backfire and spark a negative reaction from employees. People want appreciation to be genuine. Workers are skeptical of programs implemented from the top down where supervisors are given an instruction to "communicate appreciation for each team member at least once a week." While we all want to know that we are valued, we want it to be authentic, not contrived.

Second, *appreciation needs to be viewed as valuable to the recipient in order to have an impact.* This is directly related to the necessity for individualized communication. Just as individuals have a primary love language in family relationships, they also have a primary appreciation language in the work setting.

The challenge, from the supervisor's perspective, is to know what actions hit the mark and effectively communicate appreciation to a team member. This is why we developed the **MBA Inventory**, along with the specific "action items" for each language of appreciation. We wanted to develop a tool that provided accurate, individualized actions business owners and organizational leaders can use to show their appreciation for their team members without having to guess about what will be most significant to the employee. We agree with Buckingham and Clifton who state in their bestselling *Now, Discover Your Strengths*: "To excel as a manager, to turn your people's talents into productive, powerful strengths, requires an additional all-important ingredient. Lacking this ingredient . . . you will never reach excellence. The all-important ingredient is individualization."[3]

In today's current financial climate, demands on employees are greater than ever.

Third, another important research finding is that *employees are more likely to "burn out" when they do not feel appreciated or emotionally supported by their supervisors.* In today's financial climate, businesses have had to reduce the number of employees, raises and financial compensation have been slowed or halted, and the demands on employees are greater than ever. This is the perfect set of conditions for employees to become discouraged. More work, less support from others, little financial incentive, and fear about the future combine to make employees feel insecure.

We have found many organizations that are looking for ways to encourage their team members and reward them for work well done but are no longer able to use financial rewards to accomplish this purpose. This is especially true in the areas of government, schools, social service agencies, and nonprofit organizations. Directors and administrators now must find ways to encourage team members that do not require large amounts of financial resources.

Finally, there is a bit of good news for these business leaders. When leaders actively pursue communicating appreciation to their team members, the whole work culture improves. Ultimately, the managers report that they are enjoying their work more. All of us thrive in an atmosphere of appreciation.

WHEN APPRECIATION MISSES THE MARK

As previously noted, each of us has a primary and secondary language of appreciation. Our primary language communicates more deeply to us than the others. Although we will accept appreciation in all five languages, we will not feel truly encouraged unless the message is communicated through our primary language. When messages are sent repeatedly in ways outside of that language, the intent of the message "misses the mark" and loses the impact the sender had hoped for.

We all tend to communicate to others in ways that are most meaningful to us—we "speak our own language." However, if the message is not the appreciation language of the employee, it may not mean to them what it would mean to you. That is why many employees are not encouraged when they receive a reward as part of the company's recognition plan—it doesn't speak in their preferred language of appreciation.

For example, Ellen consistently leads her department in sales and with the highest marks in customer service. At their department's quarterly meetings, she is regularly called forward to receive a reward. For Ellen, this is like torture. She hates to be in front of groups and she doesn't want public attention. What she would value is time with her supervisor regularly where she could share her ideas on how to improve customer service. Ellen's primary language of appreciation is *Quality Time*, not *Words of Affirmation*. Giving her public recognition is embarrassing to Ellen and a negative experience for her—clearly not affirming.

This process of miscommunication can be frustrating to both the sender and the recipient. Consider the following scenario: "What is the matter with Mike?" Claricia asked a colleague. "I tell him he is doing a good job. I even bought him tickets to a Yankees game this weekend to show him how much I appreciated the extra hours he put in to get the project done. And yet, he mopes around here and tells Jim that he doesn't feel the management team really values what he does. What does he want?"

What Mike wants is help from his teammates when a project needs to be done. He doesn't like to work by himself, although he will if necessary. He values *Acts of Service* and would be really encouraged if either his colleagues or his supervisor would stay late with him some evening and pitch in to help him get the project done. Telling him "Thanks" or giving him some tangible gift after the fact is okay, but it doesn't really meet his emotional need for feeling appreciated.

Consider the following example related to our physical needs. At various times throughout the day, we might feel thirsty, hungry, or physically tired. And someone who wants to help make us feel better may take it upon themselves to provide what they perceive we need. But if you are thirsty for a glass of water, and they offer you a seat to rest upon—it's nice, but it doesn't quench your thirst. Or if you are exhausted from working outside all day and a friend gives you a snack but doesn't let you sit down to rest, the food may temporarily give you a boost of energy but the action doesn't fully give you the rest you desire. Similarly, acts of encouragement or demonstrations of appreciation in ways that are not meaningful to a coworker may be appreciated as a nice gesture, but one's deeper need for appreciation remains unmet.

WHO CAN USE THE *MOTIVATING BY APPRECIATION* CONCEPTS?

When we began our research, we visualized supervisors using the principles of motivating by appreciation to enhance the work relationships with those they supervise. However, as we field-tested the model across a variety of organizations (for-profit/not-for-profit, and among a variety of industries), we found an interesting response. The concept of encouraging colleagues and showing appreciation to coworkers was valued by individuals in virtually all roles and settings. Repeatedly and consistently, team members were excited about using the concepts with their peers and colleagues as much as within the context of supervisory relationships. Our conclusion is that people want to encourage and show appreciation to those with whom they work regardless of the organizational role they have.

As a result, throughout the book, you will find that we switch back and forth both in our terminology (*supervisor, manager, coworker, team member,* and *colleague*) and in the examples we use. In essence, the principles can apply regardless of the type of formal positional relationship you have with others.

This leads to the overall thesis of this book. We believe that people in the workplace (whether a paid or volunteer position) need to feel appreciation in order for them to enjoy their job, do their best work, and continue working over the long haul. Understanding how you are encouraged and how those with whom you work experience encouragement can significantly improve your relationships in the workplace, increase your job satisfaction, and create a more positive work environment. It is our intent to provide the tools, resources, and information to help you gather this knowledge and apply it in a practical, meaningful way in your work setting.

If you're not convinced that your workplace needs improved communication of appreciation, please see the resource "Picking Up Some Not-So-Subtle Cues That Your Colleagues Need to Feel Appreciated" in the Appreciation Toolkit at the back of this book or at our website (appreciationatwork.com/resources). You may also want to take the questionnaire on the site entitled, "How Dysfunctional Is Your Workplace?" This may provide a humorous but insightful perspective on your workplace environment.

MAKING IT PERSONAL

Reflect on the following:

1. On a scale of 0–10, how appreciated do you feel by your immediate supervisor?

2. On a scale of 0–10, how appreciated do you feel by each of your coworkers?

3. When you are feeling discouraged at work, what actions by others have encouraged you?

4. When you want to communicate appreciation to your colleagues, how do you typically do so?

5. How well do you believe you and your coworkers know how to express appreciation to one another?

6. How interested are you in finding effective ways to support and encourage those with whom you work and thus create a more positive work environment?

2

Understanding the Return on Investment from Appreciation and Encouragement

Business leaders, whether they are owners or managers, are strongly focused on the profitability of the business and the return on investment (ROI) being produced for the owners. In fact, ROI is one of the measuring sticks by which executives and managers are monitored regarding their professional performance. While most owners want their staff to enjoy their work and have positive attitudes about the company, ultimately business leaders assess the benefits of any program or activity in terms of its impact on the financial health of the company. If an activity—like the *MBA* model—does not add to the health of the company and at the same time may take away focus and energy, why would a manager want to try it?

Often when we share the *Motivating by Appreciation* model with business executives and organizational leaders, ultimately the question "Why?" arises. "Why should we be concerned about communicating appreciation to our employees? We pay them fairly. In these economic conditions, they should be thankful they have a job. Yes, on the one hand, I want them to be happy and feel appreciated; but, on the other hand, we are running a business here. This is not about hugs and warm fuzzies—it is about providing goods and services while making a profit."

> *"Why should we be concerned about communicating appreciation to our employees? In these economic conditions, they should be thankful they have a job."*

This response is neither unusual nor unreasonable for those who are responsible for the financial health of a business. The world of work is a demanding environment with harsh realities. Managers and directors have to deal with global competition, reduced budgets, increased taxes, and often an untrained workforce. No one has extra time or energy to waste on projects that do not contribute to the success of the organization. So, a reality-based question that needs to be answered is: "What benefits will I (or my organization) gain from engaging in a process of consistently communicating appreciation to my staff?"

In this chapter, we want to answer that question so that business leaders can determine whether or not the benefits outweigh the cost of time and energy to invest in the process of motivating by appreciation.

HOW THINGS HAVE CHANGED!

When we started this project in 2006, many reports were proclaiming the approaching problem of not being able to find quality employees. At that time, some of the chief issues facing employers were a less-than-adequately trained workforce, employees who often did not have a good work ethic, and a shrinking labor pool given the aging of the baby boomer generation.

Now, of course, employers and employees face a different world. The increasing globalization of economics and the world marketplace that Thomas Friedman first explored in his recent bestseller *The World Is Flat* has become a reality. In the past, businesses competed either with other local, regional, or sometimes national firms. However, now most companies (and those individuals looking for jobs) have global competition from businesses in China, India, Singapore, Kazakhstan, Brazil, and many other locales. Businesses are now forced to function in an ever-more-competitive environment.

Second, the economic downturn that began in 2008 has significantly altered the business landscape. The impact of the financial crisis has been felt worldwide. The US economy has shed hundreds of thousands of jobs. Many businesses and employers have had to trim their workforces just to stay afloat. Those employees who kept their jobs may have

> *The bottom-line result is that **retaining quality employees is critically important** for companies and organizations today.*

faced reductions in their benefits packages; many have gone without raises or bonuses for several years as businesses sought to retain their people while still staying financially viable. Employers and employees have both had to sacrifice in the current climate. But the bottom-line result is that retaining quality employees is critically important for companies and organizations today.

MANAGERS' FIVE GREATEST CONCERNS

When we speak to groups of business and organizational leaders and ask them their biggest employee-related concerns, here is what they tell us:

- discouragement
- burnout
- feeling overwhelmed
- losing the positive corporate culture built over the years
- how to encourage employees with few financial resources available

So maintaining positive morale among staff without the aid of financial rewards is more urgent than ever. The risk of discouragement and staff burnout is high. Employers and managers are concerned and looking for solutions.

Job security, the feeling or belief that one's employment is safe, is critical to most workers today. But no employer can *guarantee* the security of their employees. However, helping employees and staff feel wanted and appreciated can help ease their fears. The best way we know to accomplish this is through communicating appreciation individually to staff in the ways that are most meaningful to them as a person.

WHY EMPLOYEES LEAVE

When we speak to groups or consult with businesses, we often ask this question: "What do you think is the primary reason people switch jobs?" The most frequent responses received are "for more money" or "to move up—to get a better position." However, we know that leaving for better pay or moving to a higher-level position are not the reasons why most people leave their current employment. In fact, research compiled over a four-year time span by one of the leading third-party exit interviewing firms in the United States found the following results from thousands of interviews:

Belief: Most managers (89 percent) believe employees leave for more money, while only 11 percent of managers believe employees leave for other reasons.

Fact: However, in reality, only 12 percent of employees reported leaving for more money,[1] while 88 percent of employees state they leave for reasons other than money. In fact, the reasons most often cited by departing employees were more psychological in nature—including not feeling trusted or valued. When staff members feel their contributions are not appreciated and they don't have a sense of being valued by their employer or supervisor, they look for employment elsewhere.

Managers and employers need to incorporate this reality into their plans. Their business or organization is at risk of losing quality team members because their staff doesn't feel appreciated by supervisors and

> *"They couldn't pay me enough to stay here.* **The lack of support is deafening."**

coworkers. Most supervisors are not aware of this fact, and thus they focus more on the power of financial benefits to retain employees. But, as one fed-up manager told us, "They couldn't pay me enough to stay here. The lack of support is deafening."

Interestingly, Gallup reports that almost 70 percent of the people in the United States say they receive no praise or recognition in the workplace.[2] So, if the majority of employees state they receive no verbal praise at work, they almost certainly don't feel appreciated in their current job setting.

THE SCOPE OF THE RESEARCH: APPRECIATION ACROSS
NUMEROUS OCCUPATIONAL GROUPS AND INDUSTRIES

We have found that many in the world of business make assumptions about appreciation in the workplace that aren't true. One assumption is that there are certain types of career groups and occupations that are more receptive to the concept of *Motivating by Appreciation*. In fact, our experience has found this not to be the case—the issue is less about the industry or work setting and more about the business owner or manager.

We gathered a list of professions, occupations, and work settings in which research has been published regarding the importance of appreciation in the workplace. Please note that this is *not* an exhaustive list—partly because there is new research being published virtually every month.

Physicians	Attorneys
Bank employees	Public works employees
Public school teachers	Accountants
Special education teachers	Childcare providers
Manufacturing line workers	Corporate employees
Industrial workers	Government agency employees
Pastors	Business managers
Rehabilitation counselors	Information technology professionals
Social workers	Parochial school principals
Educational administrators	Baseball umpires
Basketball referees	Paraprofessional educators
Nurses	Bus drivers
Law enforcement professionals	Hotel managers

Obviously, the variety of occupations and industries that have been shown to be affected by the communication of appreciation in the workplace is vast. And the issue is not limited to North America—both multinational companies and businesses throughout Europe, Asia, South Africa, and Australia have all found that communication of appreciation in the workplace has a positive impact.[3]

JOB SATISFACTION: WHAT THE DATA REVEAL

In order to convince organizational leaders that consistent, individualized messages of appreciation to team members will help their organization become more successful, we need to start with the foundational concept of *job satisfaction*. Job satisfaction is a measurable assessment of the degree to which an employee (or volunteer) feels satisfied in his or her current role in a work-oriented organization. Researchers in the fields of organizational development and business management have devoted extensive study to this concept. We cannot summarize here all that has been learned about job satisfaction (several books have been written on the topic), but we can communicate some of the more important findings.[4,5,6]

The Tremendous Cost of Employee Turnover

Most employers and managers know that one of the greatest costs to an organization occurs when an employee leaves an organization and needs to be replaced. In their examination of the cost of employee turnover, Abbasi and Hollman state: "Labor turnover is one of the most significant causes of declining productivity and sagging morale in both the public and private sectors."[7]

Other researchers have outlined "the visible cost" of staff turnover as including the cost of termination, advertising and recruitment of new employees, candidate travel, the cost associated with selection, hiring, assignment, orientation, signing bonuses, and relocation.[8]

> *Managers consistently report that **the process of hiring and training new employees** is one of the **most disliked tasks they have.***

In our consulting with employers, managers consistently report that the process of searching for, hiring, and training new employees is one of the most disliked tasks they have. Most managers are focused on getting things done. They want to facilitate the accomplishment of the team's goals. Taking the time and energy to find new team members feels like an interruption. It is also a task that most supervisors are not trained to do. As a result, they generally don't feel competent or comfortable with the process.

There are additional hidden costs and consequences of employee turnover—the vacancy until the job is filled, temporary loss of production, the erosion of morale and stability of those who remain, loss of efficiency, and the impact on customer relationships while the new hire becomes acclimated to their position.[9]

Unfortunately, from the organization's point of view, the team members who are most likely to leave are those who are the most talented, well-trained, and have the capability to make a positive contribution to an organization. They more likely leave because there are other job opportunities available to them.[10]

In summary, turnover among employees is one of the largest controllable costs an organization has. Some researchers report the cost to the US economy to be at least five trillion dollars a year.[11] If a company can retain their quality employees for the long term, they gain an edge over their competitors through keeping costs down and having continuity in their relationships with their customers and vendors.

Job Satisfaction and Long-term Commitment

So, if employers and managers want to keep their employees, what is the best way to do this? Traditionally, employers have assumed that financial compensation and associated benefits were the key to worker retention. Although this is true for some individuals and in some industries (most notably, the higher levels of financial businesses), most employees do not leave their current company for another job primarily to earn more money. Interestingly, even in blue-collar occupations where the level of income has traditionally been viewed as the main incentive, research has demonstrated that job satisfaction was one of the key variables for the employees' level of commitment to their job.[12]

In fact, across numerous occupations and industries, the degree to which an individual finds satisfaction in his or her current position has consistently been found to be one of the best predictors of long-term employment. Specifically, low job satisfaction is directly related to high job turnover.

Sometimes, psychologists and other researchers "discover" the obvious. One such finding is the fact that a good predictor of employees leaving their job is that they first start *thinking about* looking for another job. This is consistent with

> *A good predictor of employees leaving their job is that they first start* **thinking about** *looking for another job.*

what we know about behavior in general. Most behavior (that is, actions) starts with an initial thought. That initial thought is followed and expanded upon by other thoughts, resulting in an overall thought pattern or belief system. People then start to rehearse in their mind potential actions, explore the opportunities for those actions, and eventually choose to act in the manner they have been considering.

The reason this is important to know is that *thinking about* leaving one's job has been shown to be closely related to an individual's current level of job satisfaction. Lower levels of job satisfaction correlate with a higher degree of considering leaving one's job. So, to follow the logic, if a business owner wants to keep her employees, she would desire:

- employees to have a high degree of satisfaction in their current position; so that

- employees wouldn't begin to think about leaving their current job; so that

- employees won't actually choose to leave and go work for someone else.

The obvious question arises: What factors impact employees' levels of satisfaction in their job?

Job Satisfaction and Appreciation

Since it is such an important issue, researchers have studied the predictors of job satisfaction repeatedly. Employers have dozens of job satisfaction assessment tools to choose from. Researchers have found that work satisfaction correlates to such factors as:

- Complexity of the work (the more complex, the more satisfaction)
- Financial pay
- General work conditions
- Recognition
- Being able to use one's skills and talents
- Perception that one's work is important and valued
- Quality of interpersonal relationships at work
- Coworker satisfaction
- Decision-making control
- Level of responsibility
- Workload

Thus, the following conclusion can be stated: The level of satisfaction experienced at work is significantly influenced by the degree to which the employee feels appreciated by those around them.

The desire for appreciation is not related to position. Business owners and CEOs, line workers in manufacturing, mid-level managers, and frontline service providers all communicate the need for appreciation. Neither is the desire for appreciation limited to industry or type of work being done, as we have already seen. Bankers, construction workers, teachers, financial advisors, administrative assistants, pastors, computer programmers, social workers (the list goes on)—all report that they enjoy their work more when it is accompanied by a sense of appreciation. It is not surprising, then, that mid-to-upper-level business managers frequently report that the primary reason they leave to go to another company is due to a sense of not being appreciated at their current workplace.

Other Findings

Appreciation in the workplace has become a hot area of research in a variety of academic fields. This seems to be related to the significant role appreciation plays in job satisfaction. But it also appears to be related to the personal experience of millions of individuals. We intuitively affirm that:

> Going to work in an environment where there is a sense of appreciation for what we contribute is more enjoyable than doing the same tasks (for the same money) and not feeling valued by those around us.

Also, *communicating appreciation within work-oriented relationships has been shown to improve the quality of relationships between workers and their supervisors, and also among coworkers.* One of the interesting observations we have noted in our work with companies is that coworkers (often more than supervisors) highly value knowing how to effectively communicate encouragement and appreciation to their teammates.

In one national financial firm, whose employees work together in teams across different locations, we found an eager response to *Motivation by Appreciation* from executive assistants. Janice, one such assistant, said, "Great! Now I know how to encourage and support Susan when she is feeling overwhelmed." We have found that coworkers repeatedly report to us the value of knowing how to effectively communicate appreciation and support to their colleagues.

Employees' job satisfaction has been shown to impact customer satisfaction. Think of the times when you have gone to the mall to shop and find yourself needing assistance. You try to locate a customer service employee. However, you have to interrupt the employee from talking on their cell phone or texting someone. You get this blank stare and deep sigh like you are interrupting their day. It is clear the employee really isn't that excited about being there or helping you. Your response as a customer will likely be less than positive. Research has shown that when employees report higher levels of satisfaction with their job, it corresponds to a more positive customer service rating as well. And, as

*When employees report **higher levels of satisfaction** with their job, it corresponds to a **more positive customer service rating** as well.*

most business owners know, customer satisfaction is often the difference between success and failure for a business.

In today's current economic environment, businesses have to "do more with less." Most companies have had to dismiss workers while seeking to maintain a high level of production. Fewer employees mean that businesses have to increase productivity. How is productivity increased? Most businesses in the United States are no longer manufacturing enterprises where mechanization and efficiency interventions are able to boost productivity, so other strategies must be utilized. Some researchers have found greater job satisfaction translates into higher levels of productivity.[13]

We believe that *Motivating by Appreciation* can be an effective tool for virtually any business or organization. The benefits for a business are clear:

- Reductions in employee turnover
- Improved attendance and productivity
- Greater customer satisfaction

- More positive relationships between supervisors, staff, and peer colleagues
- An overall more positive corporate culture and work environment

The good news is that the costs to an organization are minimal. The process of implementing *Motivating by Appreciation* can typically be woven into existing meetings and current structures. By design, we have developed the *Motivating by Appreciation* model to keep financial expenditures low. And we provide other resources to organizations in a manner where each organization can choose the level of support and resources they want to access.[14]

The research is clear, and our experience with businesses confirms the findings: Business owners and managers who utilize effective principles for communicating appreciation and encouragement receive multifold returns for their business on the investment made.

MAKING IT PERSONAL

1. *If you are a business manager, think of the employees who have left your organization within the last year. Did you conduct an exit interview to determine why they were leaving? (If not, such an interview might still be possible and profitable.)*

2. *If you are aware of the reasons why employees have left your company, what have you done to address the concerns they voiced?*

3. *Since employees' job satisfaction has been shown to impact customer satisfaction, how important do you think it is to discover the level of job satisfaction felt by those whom you supervise?*

4. *Has your company requested employees to take a job satisfaction inventory within the last two years?***

5. *Since "feeling appreciated" is one of the major factors in an employee's sense of job satisfaction, would you consider introducing the MBA Inventory to your employees? Why? Or why not?*

**If you would like to do so, our consultants can help you select a "job satisfaction inventory" that is compatible with your business.

Assuming you are interested in understanding yourself, and those with whom you work, and that you want to try to create a more positive, satisfying work environment, let's proceed to an explanation of the five fundamental languages of appreciation.

The 5 Languages of Appreciation

Words of Affirmation Quality Time
Acts of Service Tangible Gifts
Physical Touch

3

APPRECIATION LANGUAGE #1:

Words of Affirmation

 Jim Rennard is the type of guy almost everybody likes. He is outgoing, positive, and personable. As the leading salesperson for his firm, he exudes optimism and energy—and he almost always has a new joke to share.

Because of his personality style and his bulldog perseverance, Jim is an extremely successful salesman. Over the years, he has developed a strong client base that is loyal to the company. He continues to bring in new business and as a result has been quite successful financially. But money isn't what motivates Jim.

Jim loves praise—not inappropriately or excessively so, but what others think of him is clearly important to him. Therefore, if a client says to Jim, "Great job—I really appreciate your help in getting this project done and on time," he smiles and feels affirmed. When his boss says to one of his customers (in front of

Jim), "You know, Jim is one of the main reasons for our success. He takes care of his clients, and he makes sure the job is done right", Jim then walks out of the room with a genuine sense of satisfaction. For him, *Words of Affirmation* is his primary language of appreciation. Certainly, he likes financial success, but if he were not verbally affirmed, he might soon be looking for another company.

Words of Affirmation is the language that uses words to communicate a positive message to another person. When you speak this language, you are verbally affirming a positive characteristic about a person. As with all the languages of appreciation, there are many dialects. A dialect is a unique way to speak a particular language. Let's look at some of the ways to communicate words of appreciation.

PRAISE FOR ACCOMPLISHMENTS

One way to express words of affirmation is to *verbally praise the person.* Praise focuses on an achievement or accomplishment. So we tend to praise a colleague when they have done a quality job, or when they meet or exceed our expectations. This was Jim's favorite dialect. He thrived on praise.

> *Praise typically focuses on a specific task.*

In the workplace, this is the most common dialect. After all, the organization exists to accomplish a mission. When an employee or volunteer makes a significant contribution toward that objective, it seems right to praise them for their work.

Praise typically focuses on a specific task. "Rob, your report this morning was outstanding. I like the way you introduced the international element to the mix. I think we need to focus more effort on that, and I appreciate your bringing it to our attention."

Effective verbal praise is specific. The more you can "catch" a volunteer or a staff person doing a task in the way you want *and* you call attention to that specific task or behavior, the more likely that behavior is going to occur again. Behavioral research has proven the effectiveness of this principle time and time again. "I like the way you answered the phone in a cheerful tone and offered to help the customer resolve their concern" will probably encourage the receptionist to keep answering the phone cheerfully. Telling a volunteer, "Thanks for showing up early and making sure we were ready to go when the kids arrived," is far more effective than, "Thanks, you did a good job tonight."

> *"I hate it when my boss says, 'Good job guys! Way to go! Keep it up!'"*

It is well documented that global praise ("Good job," "You are a good student") does very little to encourage the recipient, and doesn't increase the positive behaviors desired. Numerous individuals have reported to us that global comments actually can be demotivating. "I hate it when my boss says, 'Good job guys! Way to go! Keep it up!' It is a repetitive mantra that has no meaning at all to me." If praise is to be effective, it must be specific.

While praise for specific accomplishments speak deeply to some of us, it is not true for everyone. Some prefer another dialect.

AFFIRMATION FOR CHARACTER

All of us appreciate positive character traits in those with whom we work—such traits as perseverance, courage, humility, self-discipline, compassion, forgiveness, honesty, integrity, patience, kindness, love, and unselfishness. It is likely that most of the people you work with display some of these virtues. The question is, "Have you ever expressed appreciation for these character traits?"

For some of us, it is easy to give words of praise for accomplishments but much more difficult to give words of affirmation that focus on the character of another individual. *Character looks beyond performance and focuses on the inner nature of a person.* Character reveals what a person will do when no one is observing. It is their default mode of living. If a person is honest, they will tell the truth even when it is self-deprecating.

> *When we fail to focus on **verbally** **affirming positive** **character traits,** we are failing to recognize **one of** **the company's** **greatest assets.***

While character traits are not as easily observable as specific accomplishments, they are in the long run far more important to an organization. When we fail to focus on verbally affirming positive character traits, we are failing to recognize one of the company's greatest assets—the character of its employees.

If you cannot remember the last time you verbally affirmed a character trait in a fellow employee, let us encourage you to reflect upon your interaction with them over the past year and seek to bring to the conscious mind some of the character traits you have observed. Write these down and then formulate a verbal expression of how you might acknowledge the value of one of these traits. For example, you might say, "John, I really appreciate knowing that you are a man of integrity. I can trust you to deal honestly with our finances. That gives me a great sense of security." Or, you might say, "Kim, you are an incredibly compassionate person. I have observed the way you respond to people who are expressing frustration. You genuinely seek to understand their perspective. I truly admire you for that." Once you have formulated your own statement of affirmation, read it several times until you feel comfortable in expressing it verbally. Then look for an opportunity to verbally affirm a coworker by focusing on one of their character traits.

For some individuals, this is the dialect that speaks most deeply to their need to feel appreciated. One man said, "This has been the most significant day in my fifteen years of working for the company. When my manager said to me, 'Ron, I've never told you this but I have always admired you. You are one of the kindest men I've ever met. I notice the way you pitch in and help your colleagues when they seem overwhelmed with a task. You don't have to do that; it's not a part of your job description. But it speaks deeply to me of your character'—when he said that, I was overwhelmed. I really did not know what to say so I just said, 'Thank you.' When I went home that night, I told my wife what he had said and she said, 'He's right. You are also one of the kindest men *I* have ever met.' Wow! It's a day I will never forget."

We are convinced that there are many "Rons" in every company, waiting to hear words of affirmation that focus on their character. Nothing could make them feel more appreciated.

FOCUSING ON PERSONALITY

Another dialect of words of appreciation is *words that focus on positive personality traits*. Personality is our normal way of approaching life. There are numerous personality profiles that seek to help people identify both the positive and negative aspects of their own personality. If we understand our own personality patterns, we can learn to "play to our strengths" and minimize our weaknesses.

Some of the common words used to describe personality are:

• Optimistic	• Pessimistic
• Aggressive	• Passive
• Neat	• Disorganized
• Planner	• Spontaneous
• Logical	• Intuitive
• Talker	• Doer

When a manager or fellow employee observes positive personality traits and verbally affirms them, you help the individual play to his strengths. The very fact that you affirm that personality pattern makes him feel appreciated. The following statements are examples of words of affirmation that focus on positive personality traits:

- "One of the things I admire about you is that you are always optimistic. I sometimes get discouraged but when I talk with you, I always go away with a more positive perspective. I appreciate that."

- "When I walk into your office, I am always inspired. Your desk is always so neat. I wish I were more organized. I really admire that about you."

- "I have observed that while we have a number of people in our department who are big talkers, you are the one who makes things happen. While others are still contemplating what to do, you are actually doing it already. I greatly admire that and appreciate your contribution to the company."

- "I have observed the wisdom of your intuition. We sometimes spend a lot of time trying to approach things by logic, but nine times out of ten your intuition nails the issue. I really appreciate that about you."

• "Your quiet nature makes you perfect for your job. I have noticed how carefully you listen to our clients when they come with complaints. You are never quick to give an answer until you fully understand their perspective. I really appreciate that."

If you cannot remember the last time you affirmed one of your colleagues by words of affirmation that focused on his/her personality, let us encourage you to consciously look for their positive personality traits. Within the next two weeks, verbalize affirmation for a positive trait you observe. For some people, this is the primary way that they feel affirmed.

HOW AND WHERE TO AFFIRM

Not only are there many dialects or ways to express words of affirmation, but there are also numerous settings in which words of affirmation may be spoken. Understanding the preferred context in which you affirm someone is another part of learning to speak the language of words of affirmation fluently. Here are some of the most common settings in which words of affirmation can be spoken effectively:

Personal, one-on-one

A private conversation with one of your staff can be deeply encouraging. A quick word such as, "Don, I just wanted to let you know I appreciate your hard work and commitment to getting the job done right," can be significant. In fact, the feedback we have received from interviewing individuals is that personal, one-on-one communication is the most valued and, therefore, the most effective form of words of affirmation. Managers and colleagues who take the time and effort to use this approach are viewed by their team members as being highly supportive.

Praise in front of others

Some people value receiving praise in front of people who are important to them. They don't necessarily need or want a public announcement, but calling attention to the good work they are doing in front of their supervisor, colleagues, or clients communicates "I value you" to them. Praise can be given in informal meetings with one's small team of coworkers or to larger corporate gatherings of the organization.

If the purpose of such recognition is to encourage the individual (rather than fulfill a company policy), it is wise to understand what is valued by your team member. Some research has shown that verbal praise given in the context of a smaller group is more valued by workers than large-gathering awards.

Written affirmation

Expressing thanks for a job well done through writing is easier and more frequently done in today's world of electronic communication. An email or text message takes just a minute and can be really important to your coworker who stayed late to complete the presentation. One manager indicated that he consistently texts his team members a note of praise, usually right after the presentation is completed.

Handwritten notes are still valued by many workers because they seem more personal and take more time and effort to complete. One nonprofit organizational leader confided to us that he gets a lot of direct verbal praise, "which is fine," and also numerous positive emails, "which I don't really value that much. But what really means something to me is when someone takes the time to write me a handwritten note."

Public affirmation

Some of us are not shy. We like the spotlight, attention, and hoopla that accompany public recognition of the work we have done. Having a supervisor stand up in a group meeting and recognize our leadership in completing a significant task can encourage some individuals who have worked long and hard to make sure the goal was reached. However, there are variables that make the experience more or less satisfying for the recipient. Some of those variables are whether the event is planned or a surprise and who is in attendance (top organizational leaders, direct supervisor, close team members, family members). All of these are important considerations. Knowing the preference of the person being honored is exceedingly important.

"THANKS, MISS ROBERTS!"

If ever there were a person who wanted to avoid public recognition of the work she does, Becky Roberts is the poster child. Becky is a quiet, unassuming woman in her late forties who tirelessly works behind the scenes at her church in a part-time paid position. In addition to overseeing the toddler nursery and making sure it is staffed with adult volunteers every Sunday morning, Becky also serves single mothers who find themselves in difficult life circumstances. She helps gather baby supplies (car seats, disposable diapers) for them; assists them in getting food stamps and other financial aid; and personally shuttles women and their children to medical and dental appointments throughout the week.

Becky is highly valued and appreciated, not only by the women she serves but by the pastors and staff at her church. She doesn't look for praise from others, and would be embarrassed to receive public praise or an award of recognition. But Becky *is* motivated by verbal affirmation—just a different type. She loves to receive notes of thanks from the women she has served, even if they are almost illegible, with poor grammar and spelling. In fact, Becky keeps an "encouragement file" in which she puts notes that she receives. Then when she is tired or discouraged, she pulls out the file and rereads the notes to help keep her going. The notes of thanks from the pastors or women leaders at the church are valued, but she is encouraged even more by the scrawled note along with a hand-drawn picture from seven–year-old Keisha, who wrote: "Thanks, Miss Roberts! I love you! Keisha."

Here are some ways staff and employees have told us that they like to receive verbal affirmation:

- Occasionally tell me, "Thanks for working hard."

- Write me an email and acknowledge when I have done a good job.

- Acknowledge my effort on a project, in the presence of my colleagues.

- Tell others (when I am not around) about the good job I am doing.

- Give me a specific compliment when I have done something well.

- In my review, write a specific list of the things you like about my work performance.

- Praise me in private, not in front of others.

- Write me a handwritten note of appreciation.

• Give me encouragement after I have handled a difficult situation.

• Give our team a group compliment when we have done well.

One of the values of having your entire work team complete the **Motivating by Appreciation Inventory** is that you will receive a specific action checklist so you will know not only the kind of affirming words your colleagues like to hear but also the context in which they would most like to receive them. With this information, you can be sure to "hit the mark" when you seek to give affirming words.

MISSING THE MARK: HOLLOW PRAISE

Words of praise can be encouraging to your workers, but they must be sincere. If they are experienced as being hollow or insincere by the recipient, they will not accomplish the purpose of affirmation. Unfortunately, we cannot control others' perceptions of our actions. They may misunderstand our intentions or attribute motives that are not true. However, we should seek to give affirmation only when we are sincere.

Your tone of voice can communicate: **"I'm saying these words but I don't really mean it."**

If words of affirmation are to be most effective, they must be given in the context of a positive, healthy relationship. If you are in the midst of a conflict with your staff member or if there has been any sense of jealousy regarding their success, then a compliment is likely to be interpreted as insincere. Your tone of voice (monotone, low volume, or spoken with a sarcastic edge) and your body language (rolling of the eyes, an angry facial expression, poor eye contact) can also communicate,

"I'm saying these words but I don't really mean it." If you are not able to sincerely express affirmation to your colleague, then silence is preferred until you are able to communicate with integrity and a positive attitude.

THE TRAGEDY OF NEGLECT

The greatest tragedy we have observed is that while most managers, supervisors, and colleagues genuinely appreciate the people with whom they work, they often neglect to verbally express that appreciation. I (Gary) had this graphically demonstrated to me. I had spoken at one of the largest publishing houses in the country when a man walked up to me after my presentation and said, "I have worked for this company for twenty years. I think I have done a good job. I have been very creative. My ideas have made a lot of money for the company, but not once in twenty years has anyone ever told me that they appreciated my work." I looked into his eyes as tears rolled down his face. He continued, "How I wish you had given this lecture for our company twenty years ago. I don't expect appreciation every week or even for every project. But wouldn't you think that in twenty years, somebody might express appreciation at least once?" It was obvious to me that his primary language of appreciation was words of affirmation, and he had never received them. I walked away from that encounter and wondered how many other employees in organizations across this country would echo his sentiments?

After reading this chapter, we hope that you will make it your goal that none of your coworkers will ever be able to honestly

"But wouldn't you think that in twenty years, somebody might express appreciation at least once?"

make such a statement. Make it your ambition to look for opportunities to give words of affirmation.

MAKING IT PERSONAL

1. *Can you recall a time within the last week when you verbally affirmed a coworker? If so, what did you say? How did they respond to your affirmation?*

2. *Have you received a verbal affirmation from a manager or colleague within the past week? If so, what did they say? How did you feel?*

3. *On a scale of 0–10, how important to you is receiving words of affirmation from your coworkers?*

4. *Choose a colleague you feel is deserving and give them a statement of affirmation within the next two weeks.*

5. *If you are a manager or supervisor, select an employee you can genuinely affirm and do so within the next two days.*

Words of Affirmation Quality Time
Acts of Service Tangible Gifts
Physical Touch

4

Quality Time

 Anne Taylor is a team player. She helps organize major events at the private school at which she works. Her official position is director of admissions, but everyone knows that Anne is also the lead person for the annual fund-raiser as well as the alumni weekend. She does an excellent job overseeing a large team of volunteers.

Anne enjoys "hanging out" with her colleagues and supervisor after a job is completed. She said, "I feel like we all need to celebrate together." So, she initiated what has become a tradition—going out for ice cream sundaes when they have finished cleaning up after a major event. It's something that the whole team anticipates. Anne wants her team to feel appreciated and this is her way of expressing appreciation.

After interviewing Anne, we were not surprised to find that her primary language of appreciation is *Quality Time*. What makes her feel most appreciated is Mr. Johnson, the headmaster of the school, dropping by her office, sitting down in the chair, and saying, "Tell me how things are going." This opportunity to share with him the progress she is making in various projects and her frustrations and suggestions is what makes her feel most encouraged and appreciated. Whether Mr. Johnson realizes it or not, these brief expressions of interest in Anne's work makes her feel a part of the team and energizes her to keep going.

> *What makes her feel **most appreciated** is the headmaster of the school dropping by her office and saying, "**Tell me how things are going.**"*

Showing staff members that you appreciate them by speaking the language of quality time is a powerful yet largely misunderstood tool for managers. In the past, many supervisors have interpreted employees' desire for quality time as an inappropriate desire to be their friend, or an effort to "get in good" with the boss in order to have undue influence and receive favors. Our research indicates that this is seldom the attitude of the employee whose primary appreciation language is quality time. This employee simply wants to feel that what they are doing is significant and that their supervisor values their contribution. It is these brief but genuine expressions of interest in what they are doing that makes them feel appreciated.

Managers who understand that people have different languages of appreciation will discover that some team members need individual time and attention to feel like they are an important part of the team. It is a wise investment to give them quality time. For those colleagues for whom quality time is their primary language of appreciation, a little time can go a long way to help them feel valued, to feel connected with the larger purpose of the organization, and to solidify commitment to getting the project completed.

Jason is the office manager in a multiple-doctor outpatient clinic. He is in charge of the administrative aspects of staffing, billing, and facility-based issues. The group of ten doctors has one leading, managing doctor in addition to several nurses and other support personnel. Jason knows that Dr. Schultz juggles a busy practice, administrative duties, and supervision of interns. Jason greatly valued the time she took each week to meet with him to go over his issues and concerns. Jason reported to us, "I know Dr. Schultz is busy—wildly busy. But she always makes the time to meet with me virtually every week. If she didn't, I know I would feel out of the loop and that the things I do really don't matter to her." Clearly Dr. Schultz's investment of time is paying huge dividends by keeping Jason motivated.

WHAT IS QUALITY TIME?

By *Quality Time*, we mean giving the person your undivided attention. We are not talking about simply being in physical proximity to another person. Many of us work closely with colleagues all day long, but at the end of the day will honestly say, "I did not have any quality time with any of my colleagues today." How could anyone make that statement? Because the key element of quality time is not proximity but personal attention.

Like *Words of Affirmation*, the appreciation language of *Quality Time* also has many dialects. One of the most common dialects is that of *quality conversation*. By quality conversation, we mean empathetic dialogue where two individuals are sharing their thoughts, feelings, and desires in a friendly, uninterrupted context.

Quality conversation is quite different from the appreciation language of *Words of Affirmation*. Affirming words focus on what we are saying, whereas quality conversation focuses more on what we are hearing. Quality conversation means that I am seeking to create a safe environment in which you can share your accomplishments, frustrations, and suggestions. I will ask questions, not in a badgering manner, but with a genuine desire to understand your concerns.

We may be good at giving speeches and instructions but weak in the area of listening.

Many managers are trained to analyze problems and create solutions. In our problem-solving, we often minimize the relationship aspect of the solution. A relationship calls for empathetic listening with a view to understanding what is going on inside the other person. Some managers have little training in listening. We may be good at giving speeches and instructions but weak in the area of listening. Learning to listen may be as difficult as learning a foreign language, but learn we must if we are going to have employees who feel appreciated. This is especially true for the employee whose primary appreciation language is *Quality Time*. Fortunately numerous books and articles have been written on developing the art of listening. We will not seek to repeat what is written elsewhere but suggest the following summary of practical tips:

1. Maintain eye contact. Resist the temptation to look at the ceiling, the floor, out the window, or at the computer screen. Maintaining eye contact keeps your mind from wandering and communicates to the other person that they have your full attention.

2. Don't do other things while you are listening. Many of us pride ourselves in the ability to multitask. While that is an admirable trait, it does not communicate genuine interest in the other person. Remember that quality time is giving someone your undivided attention. If you are doing something that you cannot turn away from immediately, tell the individual who wants to talk, "I know you would like to speak with me and I am very interested. But I want to give you my full attention. I can't do that right now but if you will give me ten minutes to finish this, I'll sit down and listen to you." Most people respect such a request.

3. Listen for feelings as well as thoughts. While you are listening, ask yourself, "What emotion is this person experiencing?" When you think you have the answer, confirm it. You might say, "It seems to me like you are feeling disappointed and hurt because you feel like you were passed over for the promotion. Is that correct?" This gives the individual the chance to clarify feelings. It also communicates that you are listening intently to what they are saying.

4. Affirm their feelings even if you disagree with their conclusions. We are emotional creatures. To ignore emotions is to ignore a significant part of our humanity. When a manager says to a colleague, "I can understand how you could feel that way. If I were in your shoes, I would probably feel the same," he is then free to say, "Let me explain how the decision was made." Because you have affirmed their feelings, you are now a friend and they are more likely to hear your explanation.

5. Observe body language. Clenched fists, trembling hands, tears, furrowed brows, and rapid eye movement may give you clues as to how strongly the other person is feeling. Sometimes body language speaks one message while words speak another. Ask for clarification to make sure you know what she is really thinking and feeling.

6. Refuse to interrupt. Recent research has indicated that the average person listens for only seventeen seconds before they interrupt and give their own ideas. If I give you my undivided attention while you are talking, I will refrain from defending myself or hurling accusations at you or dogmatically stating my position. My goal is to discover your thoughts and feelings; my objective is not to defend myself or to set you straight. It is to understand you. Understanding builds positive relationships; defensiveness creates enemies.

*Because you have **listened to them**, they will also **listen to you**.*

We do not mean to communicate that there is no place for you to share your own ideas and feelings. However, if you are trying to express appreciation by spending quality time with a colleague, the first focus is on understanding their thoughts and feelings. Once you have listened well, you can then share your perspective. Hopefully because you have listened to them, they will also listen to you. It is empathetic listening on the part of both of you that brings encouragement and feelings of appreciation to the individual whose primary language is *Quality Time.*

Sandra, an administrative assistant to a sales manager, commented to us, "I know Raphael is busy. He has a lot going and is constantly on the move, but if he would just give me fifteen minutes of focused and uninterrupted time once a week, it would make a big difference to me." Sandra is pleading for quality conversation. Without it, she does not feel appreciated.

A second dialect of quality time is *shared experiences*. For some employees, sharing experiences with their colleagues is an important way for them to feel connected and encouraged. For these individuals, traveling to conferences together, going out to eat, and attending sporting events or other activities in which they have an interest can be an important part of their team-building experience. They may not enjoy a "sit down and talk" conversation, but they feel greatly appreciated when they are invited to participate in an activity with their manager or their colleagues.

Sylvia Hatchell, women's basketball coach at the University of North Carolina, attributes the success of her teams to her understanding of the five languages of appreciation. "If I know that one of my girls' languages of appreciation is *Words of Affirmation*, then I look for ways to give her encouraging words. But if I discover that her appreciation language is *Quality Time*, I will invite her to my house on Saturday and we'll wash our cars together. It builds a bond, and she goes away knowing that I genuinely appreciate her as a person. When my girls feel appreciated, they are highly motivated to give me their best on the court."

The desire for shared experiences is the basis for off-site leadership retreats or a team outing to a sporting event. Our research indicates that men whose primary appreciation language is *Quality Time* usually prefer shared experiences as opposed to long sit-down conversations. These men tend to build relationships by doing things together such as golfing, hunting, fishing, going to basketball games, or working together on building a

Habitat for Humanity house. To be sure, they talk with one another while doing these activities, but the important thing is that they are doing something with their work colleagues that is either relaxing or making a contribution to the community.

A third dialect of quality time is *small group dialogue*. Some people do not feel comfortable talking to their supervisor one-on-one. But in a small group where the supervisor is asking for ideas and suggestions, they feel less intimidated and more likely to share their thoughts. If the supervisor listens attentively and expresses appreciation for their openness, these individuals feel greatly appreciated.

> *"Some of our most significant improvements have come out of these listening sessions. I want my employees to know I value their ideas."*

Rick Reed, president of an aerospace manufacturing company, said, "I have three hundred employees and every three months I lead small group listening sessions in which I ask them to be honest with me about what they think would improve the company. Some of our most significant improvements have come out of these listening sessions. I want my employees to know I value their ideas." This kind of focused attention where the leader is not promoting his own ideas but seeking to hear the ideas of his team members communicates a sense of value to employees. For those whose primary appreciation language is *Quality Time*, the significance of such focused attention is colossal.

A fourth dialect of quality time is *working in close physical proximity with coworkers in accomplishing a project*. We have discovered this dialect to be especially meaningful in volunteer settings. Research indicates that volunteers find their experience more satisfying when two components are involved: 1) they believe that what they are doing makes a difference; and 2) their contributions are recognized and valued by others. This often takes place in the context of working closely with other volunteers.

After the severe earthquake in Haiti in 2010, there were many opportunities for volunteers to pack emergency meals for Haitian families. Various individuals would invest one or more hours in packing meals. While working on the packing line, one of the volunteers commented, "This is great. I not only get to help the families in Haiti, but I get to work alongside other people. Teamwork always makes it more enjoyable for me." This volunteer worked longer hours than most. Had he been asked to pack food in a warehouse alone, our guess is that he would have volunteered fewer hours. It was working closely with others that made the experience feel more valuable to him.

I (Gary) was recently in Warwick, Rhode Island, two weeks after they had a regional flood. I had lunch with volunteers who work with the nonprofit organization Samaritan's Purse. They were tearing out carpet and Sheetrock from houses that had been flooded. They were sweaty, dirty, and tired, but they were energized by being part of a team working together to help flood victims.

In the corporate world, we often speak of teamwork, but those teams do not always work in close proximity to one another. Each person or group is working on a particular part of the project, but they may be working in isolation and have little interaction with each other. While this may be the most efficient way to accomplish the objective, it does not meet the need to feel appreciated for the individual whose appreciation language is *Quality*

Time. When working in close proximity to coworkers, they have opportunity to engage in conversation with one another. It is this experience coupled with accomplishing something worthwhile that makes these individuals feel deeply appreciated.

There are many settings in which managers and coworkers can express appreciation by speaking the language of *Quality Time*. In our consulting with various businesses and organizations, we have gathered from employees the different ways they value spending time both with coworkers and supervisors. Here are some of the specific activities they have shared with us:

- Go to lunch together to talk about business issues.
- Go to lunch together just for fun.
- Stop by, sit down in my office, and check in with me about how things are going.
- Take a walk together during the lunch hour.
- Come "hang out" with the team at the end of the day.
- Have an off-site retreat for the staff.
- Get together to watch sporting events.
- Go to dinner together with our spouses/significant others.
- Give me a call occasionally, just to chat.

In these and a variety of other settings, opportunities abound to speak the language of *Quality Time*. If this is an individual's primary appreciation language, he or she will thrive when they receive quality time. However, when this language is not spoken, they tend to become discouraged and disgruntled. Time invested in speaking this language of appreciation may well mean the difference between a motivated employee and one who simply does what is necessary.

Important Variables: Who and Where

As we have worked with organizations, we've received important and consistent feedback from nonmanager employees. There is a distinct difference between what they desire from their supervisor and what they desire from coworkers. "The issue of quality time is difficult for me," Holly said, "because it depends whether you are talking about time with my supervisor or time with my coworkers. Although I like my supervisor—he's a great guy— there are some things I like doing with my colleagues that would feel weird if I did them with my supervisor." Many employees would echo Holly's sentiments.

We took this feedback and incorporated it into the **MBA Inventory**—by allowing individuals to indicate whether the activity is something they would enjoy doing with their colleagues, or

> *"Although I'd love to go to a game with my colleagues, **my commitment to my family comes first.**"*

their supervisor, or potentially with both their coworkers and supervisor. We believe this makes the inventory much more valuable to both supervisors and colleagues.

When we discussed the inventory results with a team of manufacturing supervisors, another important issue was raised—*when* do we speak the language of *Quality Time*? Phil, a relatively outspoken manager in his mid-forties, said, "I have to be honest with you. Quality time is probably my primary language of appreciation, and I love hanging out with my friends. But time is my most valuable resource. I have three kids and my wife, and they come first. Although I'd love to go to a game with my colleagues, my commitment to my family comes first. So if I'm going to spend time with you guys, it is typically going to have to be connected to the workday." This led to a healthy discussion of ways to spend quality time with coworkers during the context of the workday (including maybe meeting briefly before or after work).

Missing the Mark: "I'm Here, Aren't I?"

Sometimes all of us try to accomplish tasks by simply going through the motions. Unfortunately, this can include spending time with coworkers.

The scenario is not uncommon. The tradition in many corporate offices is for everyone to go to a restaurant for dessert whenever a key team member is promoted or moves to a different department within the organization. Everyone shows up physically, but often it is clear that not everyone is there emotionally. This may be evidenced by showing up late, not interacting with anyone else, being critical of the restaurant, and generally exuding a bad mood. Most everyone is thinking the same thing—"Why did you bother to come? We don't need a wet blanket on our party."

Spending quality time with others requires a positive attitude. When you do something resentfully, out of a sense of obligation, the message sent to colleagues is not "You are valued" but rather, "I have more important things to do than being here with you." Additionally, communicating a sense of being rushed (by looking at your watch frequently), or allowing yourself to be interrupted by your cellphone, or texting a reply on your Black-Berry does not demonstrate a sense of value to others. Genuine appreciation always requires sincerity.

WORKING HARD, PLAYING HARD

Darin Wooster is a hard worker—just ask anyone who works with him. Whatever he does, he does full throttle. He is willing to work alone, with other team members, or lead a team and delegate to get the job done. Darin not only works hard; he plays hard. When he is not working, he is full of energy, telling stories and laughing, exercising (he jogs and bikes), and pursuing a number of hobbies.

When Darin has completed his work, he is ready to "do something" with his colleagues. Nothing pleases him more than for his supervisor, manager, or his coworkers to come along. He loves to go to high school football games and university basketball games, watch pro football on TV, or go fishing or hunting. He loves to be outdoors, and whatever he is doing, he likes to do with others.

Darin especially appreciates being invited by others to be involved in what they are doing. When his boss or a colleague invites him to go golfing on the weekend, or come to their home for a barbecue, or take a run together, he feels like he is a valued part of the team. For Darin, *Quality Time* is his primary language of appreciation.

Showing appreciation by spending time with those with whom you work can take different forms, but the impact on your team member can be significant. If the individual's primary appreciation language is *Quality Time*, your investment will pay huge dividends. It is the best investment you can make in the life of this individual.

MAKING IT PERSONAL

1. On a scale of 0–10, how important is it for you to receive quality time with your supervisor? Your coworkers?

2. If you felt that your supervisor really wanted to hear your ideas, what suggestions would you make?

3. When you have free time with work colleagues, do you often inquire about their personal interests? Do you wish that they would inquire about yours?

4. Have you had a "quality conversation" with a colleague within the past week? How did you feel as you walked away from the conversation?

5. Do you prefer small group dialogue or one-on-one conversation with your supervisor? How about with coworkers?

6. If you have not yet completed the **MBA Inventory**, perhaps you would like to do so this week.

7. Consider suggesting that your entire group take the inventory. Then initiate conversation when you share your results.

Words of Affirmation Quality Time
Acts of Service Tangible Gifts
Physical Touch

5

APPRECIATION LANGUAGE #3:

Acts of Service

 Margaret Hartman (affectionately called Maggie by her friends) is a fireball—the kind of worker you want on your team. She has lots of energy, works hard, and is extremely efficient. She is a team leader and able to get her colleagues excited about completing the project.

Maggie doesn't work for praise or recognition. She has a caring attitude, and she intrinsically enjoys working and seeing tasks completed. Therefore, praising her or giving attention to her accomplishments really does not motivate her.

What really encourages Maggie is when others pitch in and help her get things done. She views herself as being "technically challenged" and is especially affirmed when someone helps her with advanced computer work. Maggie is only four feet eleven inches tall. Another area in which she feels greatly encouraged is when coworkers help her get things that are on the top shelf. When Maggie is scurrying around and tackling a variety of tasks, she is greatly encouraged when a teammate asks, "Maggie, is there anything I can do to help?"

On those rare occasions when Maggie is behind schedule and feeling pressured, if her supervisor takes the initiative to help her personally or to assign other teammates to assist her, she is genuinely encouraged. This is especially true if the assistance is given without her having to ask for it. Maggie's primary language of appreciation is *Acts of Service*. When others reach out to help, she feels appreciated.

*Collegiality in the workplace— **helping one's team members**—leads to more **successful organizations**.*

For people like Maggie, demonstrating appreciation through acts of service communicates caring. These individuals have the perspective: "Don't tell me you care; show me." For them, actions speak louder than words. Therefore, giving them a gift or verbal praise can often be met with indifference. They are thinking, "What I could really use is a little help."

While many people in our culture are motivated to get involved in social service projects, the idea of serving someone in the world of work is a foreign concept to them. Part of this is explained by the individualistic environment within many work settings. People have clearly delineated roles, tasks, and responsibilities. While we agree with and support the need for workers being held accountable for their responsibilities, we also believe that collegiality in the workplace—helping one's team members—leads to more successful organizations.

When our focus is on "getting ahead" personally or reaching

one's goals regardless of the impact on others, internal tension often sabotages growth. True leadership requires a willingness to serve others—either one's customers or one's colleagues. When others know someone is working as hard as they can and they are still behind, if a colleague or manager assists that worker in getting the task done, it can be extremely encouraging to the worker and to the staff as a whole.

I (Paul) once worked in an office in which a number of people pulled together to produce a large and complex presentation. To complete the task, it took the combined effort of financial advisors, graphic designers, technical writers, computer technicians, and administrative assistants. We had a major presentation to complete by the next morning that included PowerPoint as well as a large amount of printed material to be delivered in three-ring binders. We were behind schedule, but all of the team members, including the president of the company, stayed late to complete the task. It was a team-building experience. Each individual sacrificed for the benefit of the whole. We had a deep sense of satisfaction when the task was completed. (We also realized that we did not want to repeat the experience, so we retooled our process to make sure it didn't happen again.)

HOW TO SERVE EFFECTIVELY

Providing assistance to one's colleagues is a powerful expression of appreciation, especially to the individual whose primary appreciation language is *Acts of Service*. Such acts of service will normally be viewed as beneficial. However, several strategies can make the process more effective:

Make sure your own responsibilities are covered before volunteering to help others. Some people are so interested in helping others that they tend to "leave their post" (to use a military concept) and not complete their own work. This is analogous to the elementary school student who wants to help others get their homework done but doesn't get his own work completed. While this may be viewed as a noble act, it does not get the student a passing grade.

In the work setting, most jobs are interrelated. When one job is left incomplete, it frustrates the entire process. Your otherwise well-intentioned effort to help a coworker may be viewed as shirking your responsibilities. On the other hand, one employee may complete his task before others. When he uses the time as an opportunity to help a coworker, rather than taking a personal break, it will likely be viewed as a sincere act of service.

Ask before you help. It is always critical to ask first when considering helping a colleague. Even when you know an individual's primary language of appreciation is *Acts of Service*, you need to check with them first to see if they would like assistance on the current task. If you dive in to help on a task when the coworker does not want help, it can create tension rather than encouragement.

One worker said, "I usually appreciate the help of a colleague, but in certain situations I would rather do it myself. If someone wants to help me, I would prefer that they simply ask, 'Would you like me to help you with that?' I will be happy to give them an honest answer." If you want your acts of service to be received as an expression of appreciation, it's always better to ask before helping.

Serve voluntarily. For an act of service to be encouraging to a colleague, the action needs to be offered voluntarily. An act of service done under the duress of a supervisor ceases to become an expression of appreciation; it becomes simply an act of duty or obedience. If a supervisor desires someone to help a team member complete a task, the process will more likely be effective if the supervisor makes a request rather than a demand. "Anita, would you mind helping Mary finish that project? We really need to get it done today; I'm not sure she will be able to do it without some help." Anita is now free to say, "I'd be happy to" or, "I will if you want me to, but the last time I helped her I felt like she was taking advantage of me." The supervisor then has an option. She can pressure Anita to help, and thus make it an act of obedience or she can say, "Okay. I appreciate your sharing that with me. Let me ask someone else."

She then looks for a willing helper. She also has valuable information about the relational dynamics between Anita and Mary. If an act of service is to express genuine appreciation, it must be done voluntarily.

> *If you choose to **help a coworker,** make sure you are able to do the task **with a positive, cheerful attitude.***

Check your attitude. There is an ancient proverb that says, "Work done with a cheerful attitude is like rain falling on the desert." We think the opposite is also true. Work done with a negative attitude is like a tornado blowing through the desert. Receiving help from someone who is grumpy or who resents having to help is not encouraging. Most people would rather do the work themselves than to work around a colleague who has a critical attitude. If you choose to help a coworker, make sure you are able to do the task with a positive, cheerful attitude.

If you are going to help, do it their way. Individuals whose personalities tend to be perfectionist resist the help of coworkers because they know they will not do the work to their satisfaction.

So when helping out a colleague, it is important to clarify how they want the task done. If you want your efforts to be appreciated, you must be willing to do it in such a way that the individual you are helping will feel that the task was "done right." Before you begin to help, you may want to ask, "How would you like me to do this?"

This issue is repeatedly reinforced to us by a familiar group of employees—administrative assistants. Whether they work for a school principal, an insurance agent, or the president of a construction company, when they hear us state the "do it their way" principle, they react intensely—rolling their eyes, shouting "You've got that right!" and shaking their heads in frustration. Many times we have been told, "If they aren't going to do it the way I want, I would rather they just let me do it myself."

Complete what you start. For those individuals for whom acts of service is important, one way to *not* encourage them is to start a task and then leave it incomplete. If you are going to "help," make sure you get the task done. I (Gary) once had a coworker who volunteered to organize my library. I was thrilled. I thought to myself, "Finally, I will be able to locate a book when I need it." However, my enthusiasm was short-lived when, in the middle of the task, my "good Samaritan" informed me that because of other responsibilities she would not be able to continue the project. To this day, I still have difficulty finding the books I'm looking for.

There is one exception to this principle: Before you begin, communicate the limits on your time. You might say, "I have two hours Friday afternoon that I would be willing to devote to help get the boxes in the storage room organized. I'm not sure I would be able to complete the task, but if you would like, I'm willing to invest those two hours in at least getting the process started." If the person you are trying to help accepts your limited offer, they will likely view it as a genuine act of service.

Christie, a supervisor in an electrical components firm, recently reported in one of our *Motivating by Appreciation* training sessions that one of her colleagues had performed a meaningful act of service. Christie was on the phone commenting to one of her vendors how she wasn't sure how she was going to get all the parts orders entered and processed by the end of the day because she was so overwhelmed. When she hung up, her colleague came to Christie and said, "I overheard your comment about being overwhelmed as I walked by. Is there something I can do to help you get caught up? I could help you some over the lunch hour." They worked together over the lunch hour getting the pile of paperwork done and Christie reported, "She didn't have to do that—she works in a different department and it wasn't her job, but it *really* encouraged me."

OFFICES, ASSEMBLY LINES, AND OTHER SETTINGS

How you "help out" a colleague really is situation-specific. It depends on the work setting. A medical office, the food bank warehouse, or a traditional business office would each have its own list of *Acts of Service* that might be helpful. The type of help you give is also influenced by the role of the staff member. A particular act of service that you render may be different when offered to an administrative assistant, the department head, or a team member with equal responsibility.

Manufacturing firms and assembly factories create some unique challenges in utilizing *Acts of Service* as a language of appreciation. In working with floor supervisors of production companies, the issue of helping out workers who are falling behind on the assembly line is a complicated dilemma. On the one hand, supervisors should not "rescue" a worker who is not carrying their weight. On the other hand, there are times when the production process hasn't been fully refined and bottlenecks occur, where certain parts of the assembly process take longer than others. Part of a production supervisor's role is to identify these bottlenecks and reallocate resources (workers, machines, supplies) to the area that is slowing down the overall process. In this setting, providing extra workers to help out is not really an act of service; it is good management.

We have observed floor supervisors pitching in for brief periods of time (five to ten minutes), working alongside their team members to help the line workers get caught up and not become overwhelmed. When this service is accompanied by comments like, "You are doing a good job. I know you are working as hard as you can. We'll get this fixed so the line will flow more smoothly," it can be a great encouragement to your team members.

HOW TO HELP: SUGGESTIONS FROM THE WORKPLACE

From our work with a variety of companies and organizations, we have received the following examples of specific actions supervisors and coworkers can do that may encourage others:

- Stay after hours to help me complete a project.
- Offer to do some menial task that will allow me to focus on higher priorities.
- Volunteer to do work for me that I dislike doing.
- Help me to get my computer to work more efficiently.
- Assist me in cleaning up equipment at the end of the day.
- Bring me or my team some food when we are working long hours to complete a project.

• Provide extra time for support staff to help me get caught up in my filing and paperwork.

If you know your colleague's primary language of appreciation is *Acts of Service*, then discovering the specific service that would be most meaningful to them may be as easy as asking the question, "Is there anything I could do for you that would make your work easier?" Their answer to that question may surprise you, but you will now have valuable information on how you can most effectively express appreciation to that particular individual.

MISSING THE MARK: BEGRUDGING SERVICE

As we mentioned earlier, the most common way to miss the mark in expressing appreciation by serving others is to provide the service with a negative attitude. If the recipient of the service senses resentment or feels you are doing the task in a begrudging manner, your presence will likely demotivate them rather than encourage them.

Those individuals for whom acts of service are important do not simply want to finish the task; they value the cheerful attitude and a spirit of willing sacrifice on the part of those who help them. Don't forget to have an "attitude check" before you offer to help a colleague.

Don't forget to have an "attitude check" before you offer to help a colleague.

Leave any feelings of stress, reluctance, or obligation at the door before you go out to help others. Sincere acts of service must grow out of a genuine effort to help others.

JIM JOHNSTON: APPRECIATION IN ACTION

Jim is a low-key kind of guy—not real flashy, the kind of person that you wouldn't pick out in a crowd. But he is "there" consistently. At the nonprofit where he volunteers, Jim is never the leader or the "up front" guy. However, he is always one of the first individuals to arrive on Saturday morning to help cook breakfast for the residents of the homeless shelter. If it has snowed, he shows up early to shovel the walk. He typically does the tasks that are demanding physically, take a lot of time, and aren't a lot of fun to most people. He washes the pots and pans after breakfast, vacuums the dining hall, and takes the van to pick up food at the food bank.

Jim doesn't expect praise. He lives simply and doesn't really value "things." Nor does he enjoy going out to eat or attending special activities with others. He would prefer to work by himself. Trying to keep the conversation going makes him feel uncomfortable.

However, when Jim's volunteer coordinator shows up on a Saturday morning and works alongside him—cooking, serving up the food, and cleaning the kitchen afterward (without engaging in a lot of chit-chat), Jim knows that his supervisor values and appreciates the work he does. He doesn't want others to say "Thanks"; he likes to "see" appreciation by others helping him get the work done. That is important to him. Clearly, Jim's primary language of appreciation is *Acts of Service*.

Demonstrating your appreciation for those with whom you work by serving them can be a very low-key, yet effective way of encouraging coworkers. If *Acts of Service* is the primary appreciation language of an individual, then they are energized when colleagues volunteer to help them. When they feel appreciated, they are deeply motivated to continue using the abilities they have for the benefit of the organization.

MAKING IT PERSONAL

1. *On a scale of 0–10, how important to you are acts of service?*

2. *What is one act of service someone has done for you in the past week? How did it make you feel?*

3. *What is an act of service you did for a coworker in the past week? How do you think it made them feel?*

4. *If you are a manager, consider asking the following question to someone you supervise. "Is there anything I could do for you that would make your work easier?" If you can do what they request, why not?*

5. *Consider asking the same question of a colleague.*

6. *Workers who help each other create a positive, encouraging work climate that benefits everyone. Look for opportunities this week to help a coworker.*

Words of Affirmation Quality Time
Acts of Service **Tangible Gifts**
Physical Touch

6

Tangible Gifts

 John enjoys his work. He is the plant manager for a firm that manufactures athletic equipment— helmets for football, baseball, and biking; soccer shin guards; football shoulder pads; and padding of various types for hockey, lacrosse, and other sports. Through the years, John has worked his way from a machine operator, to shift supervisor, to department foreman, and he has been plant operations manager for five years.

John works for a family-owned business and is considered a valued long-term loyal employee. He gets paid well and generally enjoys his job. He appreciates the "attaboys" and the "high fives" he sometimes receives from his boss when the plant is running smoothly.

But what really makes John feel valued is when his boss shares with him some of the company's tickets to sporting events. Two or three times a year he is offered tickets to see some of the local teams play—the Chicago White Sox, some Bulls tickets in the winter, or football tickets to see a game at Northwestern University. He especially appreciates being able to go to the Ohio State game since he grew up in Ohio.

Sharing the tickets is not a big deal to the family owners, but it means a lot to John when he can take his son to a game, or go with a couple of buddies. Since the family doesn't share tickets too often with nonfamily members, the fact that they give them to John makes him feel genuinely appreciated. Obviously, John's primary language of appreciation is *Tangible Gifts*.

THE POWER OF TANGIBLE GIFTS

Giving the right gift to a person who appreciates tangible rewards can send a powerful message of thanks, appreciation, and encouragement. Conversely, giving a gift to someone who doesn't really appreciate gifts has little impact; the wrong gift can actually create an offense. The challenge of giving the correct gift to the right person is a primary reason why many employers no longer give gifts for Christmas, for work anniversaries, or birthdays. However, to totally eliminate the giving of gifts as an expression of appreciation leaves many employees feeling unappreciated.

Julie, who manages the office at a dental practice, said, "Verbal praise is nice. As for *Quality Time*, I don't really care to spend time with most people at work (with the exception of a couple of close friends). Nor does having someone pitch in to try to help me with my work make me feel appreciated. I would prefer to do the work myself. However, give me a gift certificate to go out for a nice meal or tickets to the theater—that is something special."

When we introduce the concept of showing appreciation to employees through tangible gifts, many people's eyes light up and they say, "Yes. Show me the money!" But we are not talking about raises or bonuses. Certainly, most people will appreciate a raise or extra cash, but in many work settings, this is not a realistic option.

Financial compensation is usually tied directly to job descriptions and reaching agreed-upon performance levels. Additionally, most organizations can't afford to reward good employee performance with financial rewards that add up over time. Remember, a raise continues from that date forward. In today's economy, most employees are not expecting a huge raise; they are grateful to have a job. However, they still desire to feel appreciated. In volunteer settings such as working for a nonprofit organization, serving at one's church, or feeding the homeless, giving monetary gifts to volunteers usually is not appropriate. It doesn't look right to give volunteers a card of thanks with a twenty-dollar bill in it when you are serving a holiday meal to homeless families. The focus of this appreciation language is primarily on nonmonetary gifts.

> *Most organizations can't afford to **reward good employee performance** with financial rewards that **add up over time.***

GIFTS: THE WHO AND THE WHAT

There are two key components necessary for tangible rewards to be truly encouraging to those who receive them:

First, you need to give gifts primarily to those individuals who appreciate them. If receiving gifts is the least important language of appreciation to an employee, then you will be far better off to speak their primary appreciation language. While a gift is extremely important to some individuals, it provides very little affirmation to others. The message of this book is that if you want employees to feel appreciated, you must speak their primary appreciation language. If it is gifts, then you want to give the kind of gifts that would be meaningful to the individual.

If you buy a gift at Christmas for all of your staff members, some of them will value the gift more than others. You may find that some will actually give the gift away because it was not something that was meaningful to them. As the gift giver, you may feel like your efforts were a waste of time and money. It is far better to identify those staff for whom *Tangible Gifts* is their primary or secondary language of appreciation and then find the right kind of gift for them.

The second key component for an effective expression of appreciation through Tangible Gifts *is: You must give a gift the person values.* Two tickets to the ballet are not going to make some guys feel warm and fuzzy. The idea of sitting in the cold on a Sunday afternoon at a professional football game literally will leave many women cold just thinking about it. However, if you can match the ballet tickets with an employee who enjoys the ballet, you have expressed appreciation in a way they will long remember. The same is true of the football tickets. If you are a manager, you may be thinking, "This is too difficult. I don't have time to figure out who wants what. Therefore, it is easier not to give gifts at all." We understand the frustration, but to jump to that conclusion will leave some employees feeling deeply unappreciated.

The critical nature of giving the right gift to the right person is the reason we created the Action Checklist for the *Motivating by Appreciation Inventory*. Although it is helpful to know that an individual's primary or secondary language of appreciation is *Tangible Gifts*, it still leaves the gift giver with a dilemma of which gift to give.

However, when a supervisor knows what gifts would be valued by the individual, they now have the information needed to express appreciation to the employee. We have found that managers and supervisors are eager to invest time, effort, and money to get a gift when they know it will be meaningful to the recipient. The Action Checklist takes the guesswork out of gift giving.

MORE THAN A MUG

Those who do not understand the true spirit of gift giving often miss the mark in their attempts to give gifts to others. They fail to understand that it is not solely receiving a gift that matters. Rather, showing appreciation through tangible gifts is effective when the gift shows that the giver has spent time and energy thinking about the gift. They have answered the questions, "What would this person enjoy? What are their interests? What would make them feel special and appreciated?"

> *Thoughtless gifts not only **miss the mark** but also **communicate a negative** message.*

Conversely, thoughtless gifts—those gifts bought hastily in response to tradition or a feeling of obligation—with no real personal investment of time or reflection not only miss the mark but also communicate a negative message. The gift seems to be a perfunctory act and not a real expression of appreciation. Such gifts do little to improve relationships. Many companies give coffee mugs, calendars, pens with company information, or similar gifts to their clients or customers. While this may be good publicity for the company, these are not generally seen as gifts of appreciation. If you want a customer to feel appreciated, it is far better to give them something that you know they would appreciate. Does it take more time and effort to give such thoughtful gifts? Certainly. One way to get valuable information is to give a survey to your clients or customers, asking questions such as:

- Who are some of your favorite musical artists?
- What is your favorite magazine?
- What are some of your favorite leisure activities?
- Who are your favorite sports teams?
- Which are your favorite restaurants?
- What events do you enjoy attending?

With this information, you are far more likely to give a gift that your customer would appreciate.

When we talk about tangible gifts as a means of showing appreciation to coworkers, it is important to clarify that this does not always mean a "thing." In fact, more often than not, the gifts that people appreciate fall in the category of "experiences" rather than things. These types of gifts include:

- Tickets to sporting events (basketball, baseball, hockey, football)
- Gift cards to restaurants
- Tickets to cultural events (theater, major art exhibit, the symphony)
- Small vacations/retreats (a weekend at a bed-and-breakfast)
- Certificates to a spa, for a manicure, or a free round of golf at the local country club

• Shopping "bucks" at a local mall
• Gift cards to a housewares store or athletic retailer

It is these kinds of gifts that are more popular among contemporary employees. (Please see "The Art of Giving a Gift without Buying a 'Thing'" in the Appreciation Toolkit at the back of this book and also at our website: appreciationatwork.com/resources.)

One challenge that occurs for some supervisors and managers is finding the time to buy gift cards or coupons for events. Fortunately, many of these can be purchased online. But for those who supervise or work in situations where they are not able to easily access the Internet during the day, buying gifts can take extraordinary effort (and thus, may not occur). And being candid, many supervisors do not have a lot of extra money to personally fund buying $25 and $30 gift cards for their staff.

In one factory setting, we worked with the company's leadership to solve this problem. The management team agreed that they wanted to support their supervisors in encouraging the company's line workers through the use of tangible gifts. So they set aside a special fund (at first just $500 as a trial), and directed the human resources director to work with the supervisors to find out what kind of gift cards or event tickets the employees would like. The HR director then purchased the gifts and had them available for supervisors to utilize with their team members. However, the supervisors were required to send a handwritten note along with the gift, to ensure that it was personalized and gave evidence of time and effort on their part. The supervisors appreciated the practical and financial support from the company, and the employees were openly excited to receive gifts of encouragement that were meaningful to them.

AN ASIDE: "TIME OFF" AS A GIFT

One issue we are frequently asked about is: "What about getting some time off? Where does that fit in the *Motivating by Appreciation* model?" This question is more likely to come from younger workers (Gen X, Gen Y, and Millennial) since this group places a high value on free time.

> One issue **we are frequently asked** about is: "What about **getting some time off?**"

In discussing this issue with the younger workers as well as business owners and managers, time off seems to fit best within the category of a benefit they receive. It is a gift. Being given the privilege of leaving work early or getting some time off when a large project is completed can be an extremely effective gift.

MARIA: NO TIME TO SHOP

Maria loves to shop. However, Maria is frugal. She has two kids in college and holds a responsible position as head of the customer relations department for a financial services firm. Finding time to shop is a challenge for her.

When her supervisor, Jermaine, found out that receiving gifts was important to Maria and that she was a frustrated shopper with no time to shop, he arranged to give her a day off (with pay) along with a $50 gift certificate to the shops in the largest mall in the area. You would have thought he was giving a child with a sweet tooth unlimited access to an ice-cream shop and telling her to "eat up!" Maria was elated. She eagerly looked forward to and planned out the shopping day and talked about her experience for weeks. In her mind, Jermaine was the best manager she had ever worked for. She was strongly motivated to do her best on the job.

That is the power of giving tangible gifts to those who appreciate them. When you find the right type of gift for the person, they feel encouraged and energized to continue to give their best.

WHAT ABOUT GIFTS FOR COWORKERS?

In most of this chapter, we have been talking about gifts given by supervisors or managers to those who work for them. However, gift giving among coworkers is just as valuable. If you know that receiving gifts is the primary language of appreciation of a fellow worker and you choose a gift that you know they would appreciate, you are building a friendship that will in turn create a more positive work climate. Sometimes, coworkers even pool their monies to buy a gift for a fellow employee when they know it is a gift she or he would highly value. This highlights the importance of coworkers sharing with each other the results of their **Motivating by Appreciation Inventory** and the Action Checklist. With this information, coworkers will know exactly what kind of gift would be meaningful to each individual. They will also know those workmates for whom receiving gifts is the least important in terms of feeling appreciated. We believe this valuable information will help colleagues create a climate of appreciation in a very genuine and meaningful manner.

MAKING IT PERSONAL

1. On a scale of 0–10, how important to you is receiving gifts?

2. If you said 7 or above, what kind of gifts do you most appreciate?

3. What gifts have you received from coworkers or your supervisor in the past year? How did you feel upon receiving the gift?

4. What gifts have you given to colleagues during the past year? How did the person who received the gift respond?

5. Do you have a coworker you especially appreciate? Do you observe them giving gifts to others? If so, you may want to ask, "If I wanted to give you something that would express my appreciation for you, what kind of gift would you really appreciate?" Or listen to their comments in normal conversation. When they say, "I'd like to have one of these," make a note and let it guide your gift purchase.

Words of Affirmation Quality Time
Acts of Service Tangible Gifts
Physical Touch

APPRECIATION LANGUAGE #5:

Physical Touch

 If you have taken the **Motivating by Appreciation Inventory**, you probably observed that Appreciation Language #5: *Physical Touch* is not included. There is a reason for this. When we first started investigating how best to apply the love languages to work-oriented relationships, we utilized all five of the love languages even though we knew it would be a challenge to translate the language of touch appropriately.

Since we had decided to start the *Motivating by Appreciation Project* by developing an assessment tool, the first step was to generate appropriate actions that communicate appreciation through touch in the workplace. We then translated these actions into questionnaire items.

Initially, it was relatively easy to create items related to touch that are culturally acceptable and that do not have a high probability of being interpreted as inappropriate. However, as we progressed, we discovered that the number and variety of these actions are fairly limited.

We attempted to create questionnaire items that would be sensitive to cultural norms but that were also meaningful in work settings. Some of the questions included:

- "I feel important when someone gives me a firm handshake as a means of communicating 'Job well done.'"
- "I feel appreciated when someone gives me a 'high five' when I have done a good job."
- "A simple pat on the back by a supportive friend inspires me to persevere through a difficult task."
- "I know I am appreciated when a coworker stands by me and puts their hand on my shoulder while giving me a verbal compliment."
- "When a personal tragedy occurs, I appreciate a hug from a coworker."

There are other displays of physical touch that may be acceptable expressions of appreciation. However, the appropriateness of these actions depends on the person, the type of work relationship, and the organizational subculture in which it occurs. Some actions are fine for certain individuals but would make others feel uncomfortable. Recognizing these variables, the challenge is to find appropriate expressions of physical touch in work-based relationships.

We know that physical touch is a normal part of life. For example, recently I (Paul) was having lunch with a friend and we were discussing this issue. He stated, "It is a tough one. You can't leave touch out completely. I just left my office and when I found out my assistant had finished a long-term project this morning, I spontaneously put my hand up for a 'high five' to celebrate. She finished the high five, we laughed, and I moved on."

At the same time, we know that physical touch in the workplace can be problematic. When we did field testing on the questionnaire, managers, supervisors, and workers repeatedly expressed concern about physical touch in the workplace. Comments from business supervisors included: "I understand the value of the 'touch' language but the touch items make me nervous." "I could see including the 'touch' items in some settings, but I think they could create problems in others."

Additional field testing of the inventory revealed that not one person was found to have *Physical Touch* as their primary language of appreciation in the workplace. Frequently, it was the least important language for respondents. So, it seemed that when compared to the other four languages of appreciation, physical touch was clearly less important to most individuals in their relationships at work. Therefore, based on our data, we focused the items of the *Motivating by Appreciation Inventory* and our consulting with organizations on only four languages of appreciation.

IS THERE A PLACE FOR *PHYSICAL TOUCH* IN A WORK SETTING?

While we have had unanimous support from all the businesses and organizations with which we have utilized the *Motivating by Appreciation* model, many people have asked, "Is there any place for physical touch in the workplace?" This question seems to be most often asked by those who value physical touch in their personal relationships.

> *Many individuals have asked, "Is there any place for physical touch in the workplace?"*

We believe there *is* a role for appropriate touch in work-oriented relationships. My (Gary's) academic background is cultural anthropology. In every culture there are appropriate and inappropriate touches between members of the opposite sex, and appropriate and inappropriate touches between members of the same sex.

Appropriate physical touches are a fundamental aspect of human behavior. In the area of child development, numerous research projects have come to the same conclusion: Babies who are held, hugged, and touched tenderly develop a healthier emotional life than those who are left for long periods of time without physical contact. The same is true of the elderly. Visit a nursing home and you will find that the residents who receive affirming touches have a more positive spirit and generally do better physically than those who are not touched. Tender, affirming physical touch is a fundamental language of love and appreciation.

What is true for infants and the elderly is also true for adults in the workplace. Affirming, nonsexual touches can be meaningful expressions of appreciation to coworkers. One young single worker said, "It's funny that no one hesitates to touch a baby or pat a strange dog, but here I sit sometimes dying to have someone touch me and no one does. I guess that we don't trust letting people know the fact that we all like to be touched because we are afraid that people will misinterpret it. So we sit back in loneliness and physical isolation." This young woman was not asking for sexual touches. She was acknowledging the emotional need to be touched. Physical touch is a way of acknowledging another person's value and can be deeply encouraging.

ALL TOUCHES ARE NOT CREATED EQUAL

The touches that make you feel affirmed may not make another person feel affirmed. We must learn from the person whom we are touching what he or she perceives as an affirming touch. If you put your hand on the shoulder of a coworker and their body stiffens, you will know that for them your touch is not communicating appreciation. When someone withdraws from you physically, it often indicates that there is emotional distance between the two of you. In our society, shaking hands is a way of communicating openness and social closeness. When on rare occasions a man refuses to shake hands with another, it communicates the message that things are not right in their relationship. On the other hand, when you put your hand on a colleague's shoulder while verbalizing affirmation, if they say to you, "Thanks, I really appreciate that," you will know that both the verbal affirmation and the physical touch have been received in a positive way.

> *"Here I sit **sometimes dying** to have someone touch me and no one does."*

Also, there are implicit and explicit touches. Touches that are implicit are subtle and require only a moment and are often given without a lot of thought. A pat on the back, a quick handshake, or a high five are examples of implicit touches and are common expressions of physical touch in some work settings. Explicit touches normally require more thought and time. An extended handshake while saying to the person, "I really appreciate what you did; I will never forget the effort you poured into this task" may well communicate your appreciation very deeply to the individual who values physical touch. A female worker who spends a great deal of time at the computer may value a neck rub by a trusted female colleague.

If you grew up in a "touchy-feely" family and touching comes naturally for you, you will likely carry that trait to work with you. It will be extremely important for you to determine whether the touches you typically give to others are received as affirming touches or are irritating to the other person. The surest way to find out is simply to ask. You might simply say, "I grew up in a 'touchy-feely' family. I know that not everyone appreciates that. So if my pats on the back irritate you, please let me know because I value our relationship."

Almost instinctively in a time of crisis we hug one another because physical touch is a powerful communicator of love and concern. In a time of crisis, more than anything we need to feel that others care about us. We can't always change events, but we can survive if we feel loved and appreciated. Even in these situations, in the work setting, it is always best to ask if the person would appreciate a hug (either verbally or nonverbally by opening one's arms as an invitation). Rushing up and giving a hug to someone who is either not expecting one or who prefers more personal space may not be experienced as supportive to *them*, even though *you* may "feel the need" to give them a hug.

PHYSICAL TOUCH AND SEXUALITY

The recent attention to sexual harassment in Western culture has highlighted the danger of touching a member of the opposite sex in a way that is considered sexually inappropriate. This type of touch will not only fail to communicate appreciation; it may result in much more serious problems as well. Ask any business owner, supervisor, or human resource manager and you will discover that sexual harassment in the workplace is a huge issue. Most larger organizations address this problem in their training of employees.

Guidelines created by the Equal Employment Opportunity Commission indicate that sexual harassment takes place when one or more of the following conditions exist:

1. An employee submits to sexual advances as a necessary condition of getting or keeping a job, whether explicitly or implicitly.
2. The supervisor makes personnel decisions based on the employee's submissions to or rejection of sexual advances.
3. Sexual conduct becomes unreasonable and interferes with the employee's work performance or creates a work environment that is intimidating, hostile, or offensive.

Unfortunately, such sexual harassment is not rare. In a study of over twenty thousand federal government employees, 42 percent of women and 15 percent of men indicated they had been sexually harassed on the job at least once during the prior two-year period.[1]

> *An **individual's view** of what is appropriate and inappropriate in the workplace **may differ greatly** from person to person.*

Some companies define sexual harassment as deliberate touching. This kind of strict guideline tends to stifle normal, appropriate physical touches in the workplace.

One of the challenges regarding sexual harassment is the issue of perception. An individual's view of what is appropriate and inappropriate in the workplace may differ greatly from person to person. This is another reason some people draw back from any physical touch in the workplace.

Our culture has highly sexualized physical touch—we believe to an inappropriate degree. Most forms of media create and send images that associate almost any form of touch with either a sexual intent or sexual response. This is unfortunate because researchers across a variety of areas have repeatedly demonstrated the positive value of appropriate touch.

PHYSICAL TOUCH AND ABUSE

Another sad reality in Western culture is physical abuse. There are individuals in most organizations who are filled with hurt and anger that sometimes erupts into destructive behavior. We see the more dramatic examples on the evening news, but many people have never learned to control their anger. They often physically abuse family members and sometimes unleash their anger on coworkers.

Physical abuse can be defined as "causing physical harm by beating, hitting, kicking, and other destructive physical acts born out of anger rather than play." The key word is *anger*. Some individuals have never learned to handle anger in a constructive manner. When they are angered by someone's behavior, the flow of vicious words is followed by physical violence. Slaps, pushes, shoves, choking, holding, shaking, and hitting are all abusive behaviors. Where this occurs, we can be certain that such touch is not affirming. Positive words and expressions of physical affection that follow such angry outbursts will always appear hollow. The human psyche does not easily recover from such physical abuse.

A sincere and honest apology is not enough. The individual who is abusing must seek help in breaking these destructive patterns and learn positive anger management skills. Explosive anger will not simply go away with the passing of time. In our opinion, when physical abuse is observed in the workplace, the abusive person should be suspended from employment immediately. Any reinstatement should be contingent upon the

> *To allow a person who is violent to continue working is to put at risk all other employees.*

individual getting appropriate psychological help in learning the source of their anger and how to handle anger in a more constructive manner. To allow a person who is violent to continue working is to put at risk all other employees. You are not serving the cause of the company when you allow abusive behavior to go unchecked.

It is also important to note that individuals who have been the victims of physical abuse in relationships are often sensitive to any type of physical contact. Although most physical abuse occurs in personal relationships and in the home, regardless of where the abuse has occurred, individuals rightfully develop a greater need for personal protection and a desire for more personal space. Often, they will react defensively to quick physical movements by others. Many times, colleagues or supervisors will have no idea that their teammates have experienced physical abuse (either in their past or in current relationships). Thus, we all need to be cautious in the use of appropriate physical touch in our workplace relationships.

BEYOND THE CONCERNS:
THE BENEFITS OF PHYSICAL TOUCH

Despite the challenges associated with touching in the workplace, we believe the potential benefits of *appropriate* touch are significant enough not to abandon this language of appreciation altogether. As indicated earlier, physical touch has been demonstrated to be critical for healthy infant and childhood development. When used appropriately, touch also has been shown to positively affect educational learning, emotional healing, and to create a sense of acceptance. Touch can communicate a variety of positive messages in relationships: a sense of trust, connectedness, and caring. Touch is a means of expressing excitement and joy.

Communicating appreciation by physical touch can have a positive impact in the workplace when done appropriately. A firm handshake of greeting or congratulations, a high five of celebration, a fist bump—all are used frequently in work-oriented relationships. Cross-cultural researchers have found that a pat on the back is almost universally accepted as an act that communicates appreciation. Interestingly, business schools have recently begun to research the impact of touch on individuals' behavior in work-based interactions.[2] We hope that such research will continue because we believe there is great value in expressing appreciation by means of physical touch.

You may wish to do a little real-life research yourself. We believe you will find that daily life observations affirm that physical touch is a language often used in the workplace. Watch how others interact when they have a positive collegial relationship. Observe how people respond when something good happens to someone in the workplace. Take time to notice the number of handshakes, fist bumps, high fives, pats on the back, and other physical gestures. Be especially alert in less formal settings such as over a meal, in an after-work social setting, or at a company picnic. You may be surprised at the amount of encouragement that is expressed through physical touch in a warm, supportive, positive fashion.

So, while we do not believe communicating encouragement and appreciation through physical touch is foundational in most work-based relationships, neither do we believe the workplace should become a completely "touch-less" environment. Appropriate acts of physical expression are valued by many with whom we interact on a daily basis and can add a depth of warmth to work-based relationships.

How do you know which coworkers would view physical touch as an expression of appreciation? Observe the behavior of your colleagues. Do they frequently pat others on the back, give high fives, or hug others? If so, you can safely assume that receiving an affirming touch from you would be received as an expression of appreciation. Typically, those individuals who freely touch others in an affirming manner are the same individuals who would welcome affirming touches from others. On the other hand, if you never see a colleague touch others and if, as noted above, their body stiffens when someone touches them, then you will know that physical touch will not be received as appreciation.

MAKING IT PERSONAL

1. What types of physical touch in the workplace do you consider affirming?

2. What kinds of touches make you feel uncomfortable?

3. Among your colleagues, who are the "touchers"? People who feel appreciated by physical touch usually are those who touch others. In what way might you reciprocate their appreciation?

4. Looking back over today and yesterday, what types of physical touches did you give to others? How did they respond?

5. If touching comes easy for you, whom have you encountered who seemed to draw back from touching? Why do you think this is the case?

6. If you have received touches from coworkers that made you feel uncomfortable, consider sharing that information with the coworker who touched you. This is the fastest way to stop unwanted touches.

Applying the Concepts to Daily Life

8

The MBA Inventory

One of the things that sets man apart from animals is his ability to communicate by means of words. Language is distinctly human. Another element of languages is that they are extremely diverse. I (Gary) remember sitting in a linguistics lab trying to phonetically record the sounds of a language I had never heard. Even when I recorded sounds, they made no sense to me at all. They communicated nothing to me because I did not understand the meaning behind the words.

We all grow up learning to speak the language of our culture. If you grew up in a multicultural setting, you may be able to speak several languages. However, the language you learn to speak first, usually the language of your parents, will be your primary language. It has sometimes been called the "heart language." Your native language is the one you understand best and the one that communicates to you most clearly. You may speak a second language or even a third very fluently, but you will always be partial to your native tongue.

The same is true when we talk about the languages of appreciation. Out of the four fundamental languages, each of us has a primary appreciation language. It is the one that speaks most deeply to us emotionally. Having heard the four appreciation languages—*Words of Affirmation, Tangible Gifts, Acts of Service,* and *Quality Time*—some individuals will immediately recognize their own primary language. Others, because they have never thought of appreciation in this paradigm, will be uncertain of their primary appreciation language. This chapter is designed to help those individuals identify their primary and secondary languages of appreciation.

The conceptual foundation of the *Motivating by Appreciation* model is based upon the core principles found in the five love languages. These foundational principles include:

1. There are different ways to communicate appreciation and encouragement to others.

2. Individuals tend to have preferential modes of being shown that they are appreciated and valued, with some modes of communication being more significant than others for each individual.

3. The most effective communication of appreciation and encouragement occurs when the message is sent in the language of appreciation most valued by the receiver.

4. Messages of appreciation and encouragement in languages not valued by the recipient will tend to miss the mark.

In short, each individual has a primary language of appreciation. Speak that language and they will feel appreciated. Fail to speak that language and they will not feel appreciated.

Being able to apply the languages of appreciation to work relationships first requires identifying your own language of appreciation. We developed the **Motivating by Appreciation (MBA) Inventory** to provide an easy, reliable, and valid tool for individuals, employers, and supervisors to accomplish this goal. Over the past four years, we have field-tested and researched the inventory so that it can provide an accurate assessment of an individual's primary and secondary languages of appreciation. The inventory will also reveal the language that is least meaningful to you.

The **MBA Inventory** is composed of thirty paired statements that compare different ways of communicating encouragement to coworkers. The respondent is asked to choose the statement that more accurately describes the way in which they are encouraged or feel appreciated by those with whom they work. From the pattern of responses chosen, the individual's primary and secondary languages of appreciation are identified.

When you received this book, you were given a registration code that allows you to take the inventory and obtain an individualized report on your responses. The registration code is printed on the inside of the back cover.

To take the **MBA Inventory**, go to mbainventory.com. Enter the registration code as your password. You will be asked to enter your name, gender, and email address (so we can email you your inventory later). Then you will be directed to the **MBA Inventory** items. After choosing your preference for each of the thirty paired statements, you will learn your primary and secondary languages of appreciation, as well as the language that is least meaningful to you.

After completing the inventory, you will have an opportunity to develop an Action Checklist for your primary language of appreciation. This allows you to identify specific actions that managers, supervisors, and coworkers can take if they wish to express appreciation to you in the most meaningful ways.

We developed the Action Checklist in response to managers and supervisors who participated in our pilot testing of the inventory. Business leaders indicated that they would like more specific information in order for the results to be practical and useful. While it is genuinely helpful to understand your coworkers' language of appreciation, it is far more helpful to be able to identify those unique actions that clearly communicate appreciation to each individual. This eliminates "shooting in the dark"—having a general idea of what is important to your colleague but essentially guessing at how to meet that need.

WHAT SUSAN WANTS MOST

Susan is a dedicated staff member of a nonprofit organization that works with inner-city youth. She works tirelessly matching adult mentors with teen protégés. She screens potential mentors, provides training for them, and interviews young people and their parents who are looking for positive role models. She then facilitates the development of what will hopefully be long-term mentoring relationships. Susan doesn't make a lot of money, but what motivates her to continue her work is people verbally acknowledging the value of the work she is doing. Susan feels genuinely appreciated when she receives:

• A word of thanks from a single mother whose son is learning how to work on cars with his mentor.

• A smile and a gentle "thanks" from a quiet teenage girl who first meets her new adult friend.

• A word of commendation from her supervisor such as, "You are doing a really good job with the mentoring program."

But don't take Susan up in front of a group and praise her publicly. And *definitely* don't give her an award for her exemplary service at the annual fund-raising event. Both of these would embarrass Susan and make her feel uncomfortable.

How would Susan's supervisor know this? She might pick it up informally or through intuition. But she might also miss this aspect of Susan's character. It would be far better to know her preferences ahead of time.

That is the purpose of Action Checklists—to give managers and supervisors specific actions that are most meaningful to each member of their team. Therefore, after your primary language is identified from the **MBA Inventory**, you will be asked to choose specific expressions of that language that are most meaningful to you.

Upon completing the Action Checklist, a fully individualized report will be generated that identifies your primary language of appreciation, your secondary language of appreciation, the language that is of least importance, and a list of the specific ways others can best encourage you based on your primary language of appreciation. You can then save your report, print it, and email it to your supervisor or colleagues at work. So, if you haven't yet taken the inventory, go to mbainventory.com, answer the questions, and receive your individualized report.

If your entire work group takes the inventory, you can now openly discuss the results with each other. Imagine the difference it could make if each of your colleagues learns how to express appreciation and encouragement in the primary language of their coworkers. We can assure you that the emotional climate, the level of work satisfaction, and the general morale of the group will be enhanced.

WHAT IF MY COWORKERS HAVE NOT TAKEN THE MBA INVENTORY?

We recognize that many readers will be reading this book as individuals. Their manager or supervisor and colleagues may be unaware of the book or the inventory. If you wish to be a positive catalyst for improving the climate of your work environment, our first suggestion is that you give a copy of the book to your manager or supervisor. Encourage them to read it and share with you their impressions.

We believe that many managers will see the value of the **MBA Inventory** and encourage all of those whom they supervise to take the inventory and will then lead a small group discussion on how they can use this information to improve the effectiveness of their communication. In our minds, this would be the ideal scenario.

If your supervisor is not willing to read the book or chooses not to buy into the *Motivating by Appreciation* concept, then you may wish to share the book with your closest coworkers, suggesting that if they would each take the inventory, they could be more effective in communicating their appreciation for each other. Your enthusiasm may spark the interest of other employees, and informally, you may spread the word and thus encourage other employees to participate. There is nothing to be lost and much to be gained in trying to lead your coworkers into being more effective communicators of appreciation.

DISCOVERING YOUR COWORKERS' LANGUAGE

If you find absolutely no interest among fellow employees but you would like to use the languages of appreciation concept to more effectively express appreciation to those with whom you work, here are three informal ways of discovering the primary appreciation language of your colleagues:

1. *Observe their behavior.*

If you regularly hear coworkers encouraging other people by giving *words of affirmation*, then perhaps that is their primary appreciation language. They are doing for others what they wish others would do for them. If you see them as being a hand-shaker, an arm-toucher, or a back-patter, very likely *physical touch* is the way in which they would like to receive appreciation. If they are regularly giving gifts to others on special occasions or for no occasion at all, then *receiving gifts* is likely their primary appreciation language. If they are the initia-

> *There is nothing to be lost and much to be gained in trying to lead your coworkers into being more effective communicators of appreciation.*

tor in setting up lunch appointments or inviting people to join them in activities, then *quality time* may be their appreciation language. If they are the kind of person who doesn't wait until someone asks, but when they see something needs to be done, they pitch in and do it, then *acts of service* is likely their primary appreciation language.

Please notice we are using *perhaps, may be,* and *likely.* The reason we are being tentative is because our research has indicated that about 25 percent of the population typically speaks one appreciation language but wishes to receive another language. On the other hand, for about 75 percent of us, the language we speak most often is the language we desire. We express appreciation to others in the manner in which we would like to be appreciated.

2. Observe what they request of others.

If you often hear coworkers asking for help with projects, then acts of service may be their appreciation language. The coworker who says, "When you go to the conference, would you pick up some freebies for me?" is requesting gifts. If colleagues are regularly asking friends to go shopping with them, take a trip together, or come over to their house for dinner, they are asking for quality time. If you hear them ask coworkers, "Does this look all right? Did I do the report the way you wanted? Do you think I did the right thing?" they are asking for words of affirmation. Our requests tend to indicate our primary appreciation language.

> *The things about which an individual complains may **well reveal their** primary appreciation language.*

3. Listen to their complaints.

The things about which an individual complains may well reveal their primary appreciation language. Brad was about six months into his first job after college when I (Gary) asked him, "How are things going?" "Okay, I guess. However, it seems like nobody really appreciates what I do and that what I do is never enough." Knowing that he was familiar with the languages of appreciation, I said, "Your primary appreciation language is *words of affirmation*, right?" He nodded his head while he said, "Yes. And I guess that's why I'm not all that happy with my job." Brad's complaint clearly revealed his primary language of appreciation.

If a coworker complains that their colleagues no longer have time for them, their language of appreciation is likely *quality time*. If they complain that only one friend gave them a birthday present, their language is likely *tangible gifts*. If their complaint is that no one ever helps them, then *acts of service* is likely their appreciation language.

Our complaints reveal our deep emotional hurts. The opposite of what hurts you most is probably your appreciation language. If you receive appreciation in that language, the hurt will likely go away and you will feel genuinely appreciated.

None of this is terribly difficult. However, it takes an observant mind-set and a desire to effectively express appreciation to others. Observing their behavior, listening to their requests, and listening to their complaints may well show you the primary appreciation language of your coworkers. Armed with this information, you will be more effective in your efforts to express appreciation to coworkers. When people feel appreciated, they are emotionally drawn to the person who is expressing appreciation. They are likely to engage that person in meaningful conversation, which often leads to genuine long-term friendships with coworkers. As a friend, they may even be open to a discussion of the *Motivating by Appreciation* concept and over the long haul, your model may inspire coworkers to join you in effectively expressing appreciation.

MAKING IT PERSONAL

1. *If you know your primary appreciation language, how did you discover it? If you are uncertain of your primary appreciation language, take the **MBA Inventory** as suggested in this chapter.*

2. *Do you know the primary appreciation language of your closest work associates? If not, which approach do you think would be the best way to make this discovery?*

3. *If you are a manager or supervisor, consider providing a copy of this book to those who work under your supervision. Encourage them to take the inventory and lead your department in a discussion of the languages of appreciation.*

4. *If your manager or supervisor has no interest in the Motivating by Appreciation concept, choose two or three of your closest work associates. Share the book with them and ask if they would be willing to take the **MBA Inventory**.*

5. *If you find little interest among your colleagues, choose one or two coworkers with whom you would like to improve your relationship and answer the following questions:*

   a. *How do they most often express appreciation to others?*

   b. *What do they request most often?*

   c. *What have they complained about most recently?*

Make an "educated guess" as to their primary language of appreciation and look for ways to speak that language.

9

YOUR LEAST VALUED LANGUAGE OF APPRECIATION:

Your Potential Blind Spot

By nature, we all tend to speak our own language of appreciation. If *Acts of Service* make me feel appreciated, then I will be known as an acts of service person. I will pitch in and help my colleagues and am always willing to go the extra mile. If *Quality Time* makes me feel appreciated, then I will often engage my colleagues in conversation, inquiring of their well-being. If *Words of Affirmation* make me feel appreciated, then you can expect that I will give words of affirmation to those with whom I work. If I appreciate *Tangible Gifts*, then I will likely be a gift giver. If a pat on the back or a high five energizes me and makes me feel appreciated, I will likely express my appreciation to others with *Physical Touch*.

Conversely, if I do what comes naturally, the language of appreciation that is least valued by me will seldom be spoken. If receiving gifts means little to me in terms of feeling appreciated, then I am likely to ignore this language of appreciation. It becomes for me a blind spot. I assume that since it has little value to me, it will be of little value to others. Thus, the coworkers for whom receiving gifts is their primary language of appreciation will feel unappreciated even though in my mind, I am freely expressing appreciation in one of the other languages. Here is an example:

"STACY SUNSHINE"

Stacy Grant is a department manager for a computer graphics design firm. She oversees the Web designers who create websites for their corporate customers. Stacy is an accomplished designer herself and, at the same time, an excellent manager. She enjoys coordinating the team of Web designers in overseeing the production process.

Stacy is a positive, supportive manager who is well liked. She has a talented team and they work together well. Stacy's primary language of appreciation is *Words of Affirmation*. She loves compliments on her work, and although she may not admit it publicly, Stacy likes recognition to be given in front of her team members and supervisor. She never gets tired of hearing what a good job she is doing.

Consequently, Stacy attempts to encourage her team members in the same manner. She is extremely generous with praise, frequently telling her team what great work they do, and extolling their artistic abilities. This is good—especially for those on her team who respond to verbal encouragement. Her communication style creates an overall positive atmosphere.

However, Stacy's least valued language of appreciation is *Acts of Service*. She doesn't want others to help her get her work done.

She would prefer to do it herself. In fact, she views others' offers to assist her as intrusive and more trouble than they're worth. The upshot is that Stacy rarely if ever volunteers to help others when they could use some assistance. This creates tension in her department among those for whom *Acts of Service* is their primary language of appreciation.

Carolyn, one of the designers in Stacy's department, is a solid team member. She has developed an expertise in interactive websites for companies that want to sell their products online. She has numerous high-profile clients. Like most graphic designers, Carolyn sometimes gets behind on projects and will have to work late to meet a deadline.

Carolyn's primary language of appreciation is *Acts of Service*. She really appreciates it when others step up and help her get a project done when she is pressed for time. Thus, she feels very unsupported when others don't offer to help. Carolyn is not irresponsible and always looking for others to rescue her. However, when she is "behind the eight ball," she genuinely appreciates help given by coworkers. When she is feeling stressed about getting a project done, and Stacy comes in and tries to encourage her verbally, the result is not positive:

"Hey, this looks great, Carrie," Stacy says as she comes over to Carolyn's area and looks at the work she is doing.

"Thanks," Carolyn somewhat gloomily responds. "But I have a lot to get done by 9 a.m. tomorrow before the client presentation. It's going to be a late night." She looks at her boss.

"Oh, I'm sure you'll get it done," says Stacy. "You always do. I appreciate your commitment and follow-through to do whatever it takes to get the job done." She pats Carolyn on the shoulder as she goes back to her office.

"Thanks a lot," Carolyn mutters to herself. "A little help would be appreciated. But no, Miss Stacy Sunshine has to run off and go around and tell everyone what good work they are doing. I'd rather see a little action and hear less chatter."

Stacy thinks she is doing an effective job of encouraging and supporting Carolyn by giving her verbal encouragement. However, Carolyn is feeling unsupported by Stacy and even resentful of her "lack of consideration." This classic mismatch of two co-workers' languages of appreciation leads to miscommunication and relational tension.

If the issue of Carolyn's feeling unsupported ever came up in conversation, Stacy would probably feel confused and blind-sided. "What? How can you feel like I don't appreciate the work you do? Carolyn, I am always giving you lots of compliments about your work. And I even took the initiative to praise you publicly in one of our team meetings in front of the management! I don't understand."

Carolyn might respond, "Stacy, I know you tell me I do good work and that I do what is necessary to get the job done. But I have to say, sometimes when I'm struggling to meet a deadline, I wish I had some help. Words are great, but actions would mean more."

And so it goes. Stacy is putting forth initiative to express appreciation to Carolyn, but not in the way that is encouraging to her employee. Carolyn feels unsupported and becomes resentful. Stacy can then feel like she is wasting her breath trying to encourage Carolyn and becomes discouraged as an effective manager. Since *Acts of Service* mean almost nothing to Stacy, she has a hard time understanding how they could be such a big deal to Carolyn.

THE BLACK HOLE

In astronomy, a black hole is an entity that sucks in virtually everything surrounding it—light, matter, energy. Whatever goes in never comes out. A black hole takes and takes, without giving back.

A person's least valued language of appreciation can approximate a black hole in the work setting. When a colleague's least important language of appreciation is *Words of Affirmation*, no matter how much praise you give them, it misses the mark. They will not feel encouraged or appreciated from compliments, notes of appreciation, or recognition in front of team members. Verbal affirmation is not important to them. You are essentially wasting your energy. The same can be true of any of the languages—spending quality time with team members, doing tasks to help them out, giving them tickets to the NCAA March Madness tournament.

Here is a fact that can save you a lot of time and emotional energy, if you are willing to accept it: A person's lowest language of appreciation *really* is not important to them. This does not mean that the other person is weird. They are simply different— different from you. The wise manager or colleague will recognize and accept the difference.

Understanding and accepting your team members' differences in how they feel appreciated and encouraged is critical to your success as a manager. If you don't fully grasp and implement this reality in how you relate to your colleagues, you will waste a lot of time and energy trying to encourage them in ways that have little or no impact on them.

Thus, you may begin to resent those team members who have different languages of appreciation. You may start to feel that they are ungrateful, negative, and don't appreciate you and all that you are trying to do for them. You may conclude that there is nothing that will satisfy them or make them feel like you appreciate their work. This, of course, is not true; thus, knowing your least valued language of appreciation and the fact that it is likely your potential blind spot is an important step in becoming an effective communicator of appreciation. (Please see the article "Why Your Least Valued Appreciation Language Can Affect Your Career the Most" in the Appreciation Toolkit at the back of the book or at appreciationatwork.com/resources.)

OVERCOMING THE CHALLENGE OF YOUR BLIND SPOT

The first step in getting past your blind spot as a manager or colleague is to become aware of it. Assuming you have taken the **MBA Inventory** and identified your least favorite language of appreciation, you now have that information. However, it is likely that you really don't *understand* this language of appreciation.

For me (Paul) in work or in other relationships, *Tangible Gifts* is my least valued language of appreciation. Certainly, I appreciate receiving a gift card to Starbucks, but it is really not a big deal to me. I can take it or leave it. So it is harder for me to put myself in one of my colleagues' shoes and really understand how they could highly value tangible rewards. I often find myself thinking thoughts like, "They certainly get excited about something that is no big deal," or "I just don't get it. I would much rather get some praise than a free day at the health club."

Therefore, I have taken the initiative to talk to some of my colleagues for whom receiving tangible gifts is their primary language of appreciation. I asked one of my team members, "What about getting tickets to the ballgame is important to you? Why does that mean so much to you?" His response helped me to see the situation from his point of view.

"Because," Joe replied, "first, it shows me that my team leader has taken time and interest to find out something about me personally and what I like. If he had given me tickets to a ballet that would have been a big-time 'miss.' I played baseball in college and still love going to games. Second, he took the initiative and effort to go and get the tickets for me. It's really about the investment he made from a time and energy point of view, rather than the financial expenditure. It shows me that doing what it takes to encourage or reward me is worth it to him—and that makes me feel genuinely appreciated."

> *"It's really about the investment he made from a time and energy point of view, rather than the financial expenditure."*

Once you have identified your least valued language of appreciation, we would encourage you to talk with colleagues for whom this is their primary language of appreciation. Ask them what those actions communicate to them and how they are encouraged by them. Try to gain a deeper sense of understanding of how they are impacted by that particular language of appreciation. It will then become easier for you to learn to speak that language with your teammates for whom it is extremely important.

CHOOSING TO ACCEPT THE INFORMATION YOU RECEIVE

It is commonly known that successful managers seek to understand the other person's point of view—supervisors, customers, colleagues, and those they manage. If a manager is unable to see another person's perspective, he will make wrong assumptions that eventually lead to poor decisions based on inaccurate information.

Thus, if an employee's **MBA Inventory** results indicate that *Quality Time* is important to them, the wise manager and colleague will take this information seriously. You may not fully understand why spending individual time with them is that important, but you do so because you choose to take seriously what they say. If you wait until you fully understand why it is important to them, you may lose a lot of time and opportunities to communicate appreciation—and you may lose a team member in the process.

> *If a manager is* **unable** *to see another person's perspective, he will make* **numerous** **wrong assumptions.**

PLAN TO SPEAK THEIR LANGUAGE

Even when we accept that other people's perspectives and values are different from our own, it is often difficult to consistently act in a manner that affirms this. We naturally tend to drift back to our own viewpoint and preferences. So a manager who values *Words of Affirmation* will tend to automatically default to giving verbal encouragement to her team members.

We have found that to be consistent and effective communicators of appreciation to colleagues whose primary language of appreciation is in our blind spot, we have to make specific plans to speak that language to our coworkers. Communicating in our least important language takes more effort; it doesn't come naturally. We must think about it more intentionally and try to look for opportunities to speak their language.

To be successful may require planning how you will show appreciation to team members who have a language that is the opposite of your own. For example, when *Quality Time* is a supervisor's least important language, that supervisor is not likely to spontaneously spend time

What we schedule, we normally do.

with their colleagues. It never enters their mind that it would be something important. So a team member whose primary language is *Quality Time* can "starve" while waiting for appreciation from their supervisor. A wise manager will take the initiative to schedule regular times with such team members. Essentially, the manager says to herself, "I know that *Quality Time* is Glenda's primary language of appreciation. I also know it is not that important to me. So, I'd better put it on my calendar to stop by and see her at least every other week to check in and see how she is doing." What we schedule, we normally do.

The language that we value least can become our "blind spot" in effectively communicating appreciation to colleagues for whom that language is highly significant. Understanding this dynamic and taking steps to correct the process can be critical in making sure that all team members feel valued by their supervisor and coworkers.

MAKING IT PERSONAL

1. What is your least valued language of appreciation?

2. Do you have team members or coworkers whose **MBA Inventory** results indicate that what is your least valued language is their most valued language of appreciation?

3. Can you recall the last time you spoke that particular language to that coworker? Would you be willing to take a moment to make specific plans to speak the primary appreciation language of that employee within the next week? If so, put it on your calendar.

4. When you speak their primary language, carefully observe their response. We think it will be obvious that your efforts to express appreciation have been effective.

10

The Difference between Recognition and Appreciation

I n previous chapters, we have talked about recognizing employees for a job well done, or when they reach a chronological milestone such as twenty-five years with the company. Such recognition is common in many organizations. In most cases, it is a sincere attempt on the part of leadership to express appreciation for performance and longevity. At first glance, it may appear that such recognition is the focus of this book. To draw that conclusion would be a mistake. We believe that there is a distinct difference between recognition and appreciation.

> *The **narrow** recognition-and-award approach has a number of **limitations**.*

One of the more popular books on the importance of recognition is *The Carrot Principle*, written by Gostick and Elton, published in 2007. Their approach emphasizes public recognition for performance-based achievements. Most of their research was done with companies with one thousand or more employees. They seek to help businesses develop rewards (largely monetary) for those individuals in the company who are high performers.

While we applaud public recognition of quality work and the importance of performance-based rewards, we believe the focus on recognition and rewards is too narrow and has distinct limitations. Unfortunately, many leaders tend to equate recognition with appreciation. In reality, the languages of the appreciation model is a more in-depth approach to encouraging colleagues than the narrower recognition and award approach, which has a number of limitations. Among them:

Limitation #1: Emphasis on Performance

While recognition focuses primarily on *performance* or the achievement of certain goals, appreciation focuses on the *value of the individual employee*. The level of performance of the employee is certainly a consideration—but not the only consideration. There are times when high-performing employees do not do well on tasks or make a major mistake. Do they cease to be valuable to the organization during this time period? Also, not all employees are high achievers, but all employees need appreciation and encouragement. While recognition focuses on what the person does, appreciation focuses on who the person is.

*Isn't there a place for appreciation **even when someone messes up?***

This point was raised by a team leader during one of our training sessions. Donna asked, "Should appreciation only be expressed when team members are performing well? Isn't there a place for appreciation even when someone messes up? Otherwise, it seems appreciation becomes totally performance-based." We completely agree with this perspective. Although supervisors want to support and reinforce positive behaviors demonstrated by their staff, workers need to be encouraged when they are having an "off day" too. In fact, we could argue that when a colleague reacts inappropriately to a situation or when they have made a mistake, that creates an opportunity for a supervisor to demonstrate appreciation for the employee *in spite of* their performance in this one circumstance. A comment like, "Matt, it looks like you are having a challenging day. Is there anything I can do to help?" may mean a great deal to your team member—and communicate that your support of them goes beyond their daily performance.

Managers also need to keep the context of the behavior in mind. An employee may be going through a period of extraordinary trauma in their personal life: experiencing the illness or death of a loved one, having relational struggles at home, or dealing with challenges with their own physical health. All these can detract from an individual's performance at work.

Changes within the organization or company may also affect the employee's performance—reduction in staff, increased responsibilities, or longer work hours can all make a difference. Challenges in the global economy may have mandated that the company make internal staffing adjustments. This sparks stress and uncertainty among employees while they are trying to figure out their new roles and responsibilities.

Managers and supervisors who utilize encouragement and appreciation can address these factors in a positive, supportive manner, in a way that programs of recognition do not. Particularly during these difficult times, managers need to be actively communicating appreciation, encouragement, and support for their team members—not based on performance or achievement but grounded in the value you hold for them as a person.

It is true that rewards do tend to motivate those who receive them to continue their high level of performance. However, they are less effective in motivating those who do not receive the reward. On the other hand, appreciation, when expressed in the primary appreciation language of the individual, tends to motivate each team member to reach his or her potential. When we feel appreciated, we are motivated to "climb higher." Conversely, without appreciation, we often settle into mediocre performance, often far below our level of capability.

Juanita, an administrative assistant to the CEO of a financial services company, reported to us, "My greatest goal is to help Eric [the CEO] be as successful as he can be—because when he is successful, then the whole company benefits. And when he is pleased with my work and lets me know that he appreciates all I do for him, it just motivates me all the more—I get a surge of energy and I am ready to tackle any problem." She concluded with a grin, "When I am doing what I am supposed to and he acknowledges my efforts—watch out, world!"

Limitation #2: Missing Half the Team

The rewards most often offered in programs of employee recognition typically include only two of the languages of appreciation: *Words of Affirmation* and *Tangible Gifts*. In these presentations, someone makes a speech extolling what the employee has accomplished and their importance to the company. Then they are presented with a reward: a raise in salary, a bonus, a new title, a gift of some sort. If the primary appreciation language of the recipient is *Words of Affirmation* or *Tangible Gifts*, they will likely feel deeply appreciated. However, for the 40 to 50 percent of employees whose language of appreciation is *Quality Time* or *Acts of Service*, such rewards will "miss the target" in communicating sincere appreciation.

Not only that, but little or no effort is given to identifying the specific type of recognition the employee being honored would appreciate. For example, we *know* that many people do not like public recognition and attention.

With every organization we have worked with on the *Motivating by Appreciation* model, we have asked the participants, "Which of you would not like to be acknowledged or recognized for work well done in front of a large group of your peers?" Not only are there always several who acknowledge this dislike of public recognition, but the intensity of the reactions is notable. We have heard comments such as, "I'd rather be shot than go up in front of a group for an award!" We believe it is important to listen to workers' reactions and comments. For many people, public accolades and a public presentation of a gift will likely be embarrassing. But some recognition proponents dismiss these concerns by saying, "They must like it because they smile for the photos." Not so! Managers and supervisors need to understand and accept that *just because* you *would like the public recognition does* not *mean that all of your team members will.*

Limitation #3: "Top-Down" Recognition
Too often employee recognition is implemented in an impersonal, top-down corporate policy approach. Employees know that the program is generated by upper-level management, rather than

> *A perception of **insincere** appreciation is **deadly** to an organization.*

being personal and individualized. Even more problematic is the skepticism this approach can create as to the genuineness of the appreciation communicated. We believe this is a critical mistake well-meaning organizational leaders make—approaching employee recognition or appreciation in terms of a managerial directive: "This is something we all are going to do."

The problem is, employees frequently ask themselves: "Is my manager doing or saying this because he means it, or because he is supposed to follow the company's recognition program?" A perception of insincere appreciation is deadly to an organization, undermining trust in communication at multiple levels.

We get significant "push back" from team members about this issue. Randy, a staff member at a nonprofit youth organization, said, "I don't want my supervisor to spend time with me just because she is supposed to, since time is my primary language of motivation. If she doesn't want to spend time with me, that's okay. But I don't want her to fake it. That's worse."

Thus, when implementing programs of recognition, organizational leaders would be more effective if they allowed team members to freely choose whether or not they would like to participate. We have found that many who are initially reluctant become interested in the process after they have taken the **MBA Inventory** themselves. We are not opposed to recognition and reward programs. However, we believe that an emphasis on appreciation and encouragement holds far greater potential for enhancing the emotional climate in the workplace and increasing the level of productivity in employees.

Limitation #4: Significant Financial Cost

Lastly, an additional downside to the recognition/award approach is the cost involved. In today's financial climate, many organizations, especially nonprofit organizations, schools, ministries, and social service agencies, do not have the funds available to pay the bonuses, large raises, or other gifts that typically come with the recognition/reward approach. And many times, the practice of giving significant financial rewards for goals achieved is not a "good fit" within the overall context of the mission and values of the organization.

On the other hand, the concepts shared in *Motivating by Appreciation* can be put to work in any financial climate, with any size organization, governmental agency, school system, business enterprises, or nonprofit and social service organization. The *MBA* approach we have outlined does not have to wait for top-level executives to approve and begin facilitating it. The program can be launched at any organizational level by managers, supervisors, or even a single employee who has a desire to create a more positive climate in the work setting.

Dave modeled this fact. He was a mid-level supervisor within his organization. He had a team of five colleagues whom he oversaw, but he also belonged to a team of supervisors who reported to higher-level managers, including the president of his firm. Dave knew of the work we were doing on this project and asked if he could have his team take the **MBA Inventory**. After doing so, we met with Dave and his team and went over the results. As we worked over time to implement the appreciation model within their relationships, he shared what he was doing with his fellow supervisors, and they became interested. Over a series of weeks, they continued to listen to Dave's stories about the project and the positive impact it was having on his relationships with his team-mates. After a while, the president approached Dave and said, "I think it would be good for the leadership team to go through this process—how do we make that happen?" And so it went.

We have seen the consistent application of individualized appreciation and encouragement within a work environment transform relationships and attitudes. And we believe that putting into practice the principles we have shared in this book can strengthen the emotional climate of any work setting.

MAKING IT PERSONAL

1. Does your company have a program of recognition for employees who have exceptional performance and/or who stay with the company for a certain number of years?

2. Have you ever experienced such recognition from your organization? How did you feel upon receiving it?

3. Describe your understanding of the difference between recognition and appreciation.

4. If you had a choice between receiving recognition and appreciation, which would you choose? Why?

5. Have you ever received expressions of appreciation from a supervisor or a colleague when you were going through a difficult time in your personal life? What did they say or do, and how did it make you feel?

6. Have you expressed appreciation to a fellow employee who was going through a difficult time? What did you say or do? How did they respond?

7. If you could make one suggestion on how to enhance the work climate in your organization, what would you suggest? Is it feasible to actually make that suggestion to someone in your organization who has the ability to make it happen?

11

Motivating by Appreciation in Various Industry Sectors

A s we have developed the *Motivating by Appreciation* model, we have conducted pilot projects with numerous organizations and have seen how effective the model can be in a variety of settings. Let's take a closer look at some of them.

NONPROFIT ORGANIZATIONS

Many nonprofit organizations provide direct services (American Red Cross, Habitat for Humanity, Juvenile Diabetes Research Foundation, Salvation Army, and many others). Others serve within their local communities—for example, organizations supporting the arts. These organizations face the constant need to make the community aware of their presence and mission, and have an ongoing need to raise funds. Staff members within these groups need continual encouragement and appreciation.

This can be challenging. While those who work for nonprofit organizations often have a sense of calling and are motivated by a sincere desire to serve others, they still need to feel appreciated. Nonprofit staff members often earn significantly less than they would in the for-profit sector. Nonprofit organizations are not known for paying huge salaries. In these work settings, the need for appreciation is critical in keeping the staff energized.

> *While those who work for **nonprofit organizations** often have a sense of calling, they still need to feel appreciated.*

Many nonprofit organizations are underfunded (especially in recent years), and the demands on the organization's staff are significant, often overwhelming. We have worked with a variety of nonprofit social service organizations: a residential treatment facility for adolescent males with severe behavioral problems, a community counseling clinic for low-income families, an inner-city mentoring program for fatherless children, and a number of church-based organizations. All of these organizations are doing good work in providing valuable and needed services to their clientele. However, they are often difficult places to work, with high demands, low resources, and not much external recognition from the community. As a result, the burnout rate for staff (and volunteers) is high. The *Motivating by Appreciation* model works extremely well in these nonprofit settings.

FINANCIAL SERVICES

Some may think that those who work in the financial services industries (insurance, investment advisory services, and banking) would not need the *Motivating by Appreciation* model.

They believe that individuals who work in this arena are primarily motivated by financial reward. While this may be true for the professional advisors themselves, their support team members need consistent encouragement as they work in a demanding, often high-pressure work environment.

We have consulted with the highest producers in one of the national life insurance groups. One of the most common concerns voiced was: "How do we keep our staff? They get frustrated with us and leave after twelve to eighteen months. The turnover rate is killing us." In meeting with the office staff (separately from the financial professionals), we found that office managers, receptionists, administrative assistants, and back-office technicians often are starved for appreciation from their bosses.

One financial firm with which we have worked is composed of high-level financial professionals and business consultants who serve extremely wealthy business families. They have surrounded themselves with top-quality team members who are self-starters, loyal, and highly competent in their own areas of expertise. However, even though they are financially successful, all the members of the firm acknowledged their need for appreciation and encouragement from one another to "keep going" and feel satisfied in their work. As a result, all of the staff took the **MBA Inventory** and continue to use the results in encouraging one another. They have also incorporated the "Action Steps" into their semiannual performance reviews. We believe that all financial service organizations will find the *MBA* model to be extremely helpful.

FAMILY-OWNED BUSINESSES

As noted earlier, over 85 percent of all businesses in the United States are family-owned. Thirty-five percent of Fortune 500 companies are family businesses. In fact, family-owned businesses employ 60 percent of all employees in the nation.

Family-owned businesses include a wide variety of endeavors: construction companies (residential, commercial, and highway), dry cleaners, restaurants, auto dealerships, manufacturing companies, car washes, real estate management companies, heating and air-conditioning contractors, banks—the list is virtually endless. Also, family-owned businesses range in size from a few employees to tens of thousands globally.

> One thing that family-owned businesses have in common is the fact that the relationships in the work environment are complex.

One thing that family-owned businesses have in common is the fact that the relationships in the work environment are complex. Often this involves family members from different generations working together. Their perspectives on how to run the business sometimes conflict. Then there are the relationships between nonfamily employees and the family owners or members who work for the company. In this complicated relational maze, the ability to communicate appreciation for work done and encouragement to persevere through difficult tasks is critical for the business to be successful.

To the surprise of those who don't typically work with family businesses, family members are often the ones who feel the *least* appreciated of all employees. This seems to be a common experience, perhaps because others see them as part of the ownership and conclude that they don't need to be encouraged.

One family member confided to us: "No one understands the pressure I feel. No matter what I do, it is not good enough for my dad. The nonfamily employees think I have it made financially.

In reality, I make less money than most of the other managers and receive no distributions from the company. If I could leave, I would, but it would destroy my relationship with my family and I don't want to do that." This woman needed to know she was valued by the other employees in the company, including her parents.

It is also our experience that business owners are one of the loneliest groups in the workforce. Given both their position and their entrepreneurial personality, business owners rarely receive much communication of appreciation from their employees. Many owners have concluded that "this is the way it is" and no longer expect appreciation from their employees. So, if you are an employee, even if your boss looks like he or she is doing fine, we would strongly encourage you to take the time and effort to communicate gratitude for all they do for the business. You might also encourage them to take the **MBA Inventory** and consider making it available to all employees.

> *It is also our experience that **business owners are one of the loneliest groups** in the workforce.*

SCHOOLS

Schools at every level of education are experiencing tremendous pressures. In fact, we believe that schools are one of the most difficult environments in which to work in today's society. Teachers and educational professionals face demands from all sides—meeting federal and state testing standards, dealing with students with learning difficulties and behavioral problems, coping with everyday classroom and academic challenges. Add a myriad of other issues with which to contend—stressed parents, divorce conflicts, drug abuse (both by students and parents), and chaotic home environments—and you have a cauldron for burnout and discouragement.

> *"I can't give them a raise, but **I can do things to help them feel** that what they are doing **is important**."*

Combine these factors with the declining funds available for resources, decaying physical facilities, and lack of pay increases for all staff, and the result is a work environment in which employees struggle with high demand and little tangible reward. This is the type of setting in which consistently communicating appreciation is vital for staff and teachers so that they do not lose heart and become discouraged.

One elementary school principal reported, "It is critical for me to know how to specifically encourage my teachers in practical ways. I can't give them a raise, but I can do things to help them feel that what they are doing is important and noticed."

An inner-city middle school administrator, when he found out about the **MBA Inventory**, became excited because it dovetailed with a program his district was implementing. The program was designed to provide training, resources, and support to encourage staff, but they really did not have a practical tool to do this. After first utilizing the inventory with his administrative team, he then had his lead teachers take the questionnaire and use the results in their weekly staff meetings. While not all of the administrative team and teachers were enthusiastic at first, we did discover some interesting findings over the next several weeks. Those who were initially receptive quickly assimilated the *Motivating by Appreciation* model into their communication with their team members. They became enthusiastic supporters of the process, encouraging others to use it as well. The team members who were skeptical but open to seeing how the model worked warmed up over time as they realized the model was not one of manipulation but focused only on communicating authentic appreciation.

College settings are also ripe for appreciation-focused managing. For those who have not worked in college or university settings, it is important to know that they are massive bureaucracies with territorial battles occurring regularly. There are also very clear hierarchies (graduate students, adjunct faculty members, faculty with PhDs, faculty members with tenure, department chairpersons, college deans), and the organizational culture is often very competitive. As a result, the organizations are not very warm interpersonally, and positive, supportive communication between colleagues can be rare. Administrators who communicate gratitude and appreciation to their staff members will quickly become effective supervisors.

This was the case during my (Paul's) doctoral program study at Georgia State University in Atlanta. The chairperson in my department, Richard "Pete" Smith, was a highly competent professional. He was also warm and caring to those who worked for him in the department. He did not let his high standards of professional competence interfere with treating others with respect and thankfulness—and he had a waiting list of staff members within the university who wanted to work for him. In all levels of education, expressing meaningful appreciation produces positive results.

MEDICAL/DENTAL OFFICES

We have found medically related professional practices to be very receptive to the *Motivating by Appreciation* model. Dental and orthodontic offices, outpatient physical therapy clinics, optometry practices, and a wide range of medical service businesses either report success when they follow the *MBA* program, or they tell us, "We need this!"

We conducted a pilot project with one outpatient physical therapy center. We included all of their physical therapists, physical therapy assistants, interns, and administrative staff. Prior to the project, we administered an anonymous pretest to each participant. We asked six questions, such as, "How appreciated do you feel in your current position by your supervisor?" and "How much do you think your coworkers and supervisor feel appreciated by you for the work they do?"

> *Another therapist said, "It seems like appreciation is now a part of who we are."*

After having an introductory session, taking the **MBA Inventory**, and receiving the results, we gave the same set of questions as a posttest. We found that the group's ratings were higher on all six questions on the posttest. This was simply the result of receiving the inventory printout, with no discussion of implementing the findings.

Then we assisted the staff in developing a plan of action to more consistently communicate appreciation to one another. After four weeks, we met to see how things were going. We had them fill out another rating scale and compare these results (post-implementation) to the prior ratings (pretest and post-inventory). The group ratings improved again across all questions.

The verbal feedback we received was encouraging as well. One supervising physical therapist reported, "This has been a very beneficial experience for us. Although we were already a positive place and we tell each other 'Thank you' a lot, going through this process reinforced and enhanced what we were already doing." Another therapist said, "It seems like appreciation is now a part of who we are. We have all started to show appreciation more often and regularly. It has sort of become like our culture." It is our desire that many medical/dental settings will discover the value of *Motivating by Appreciation.*

MINISTRIES/CHURCHES

Employees of churches and other ministries often have a unique relationship with their vocation. In addition to their job being a source of income, they work also with a sense of spiritual calling and a desire to serve others. In many church settings, employees are expected to give of themselves sacrificially, which almost always includes a lower salary than they would receive doing similar work in a different setting.

Research has shown that pastors have a higher level of burnout when they don't feel appreciated by those whom they serve. Our personal observations confirm this finding. Pastors (including associate pastors, youth and children's ministers, women's ministry leaders, and worship leaders) often feel criticized and report that statements of encouragement are "few and far between."

In our work with church staff members, we consistently find a deep hunger for appreciation.

In our work with church staff members and individuals who work for other nonchurch ministries, we consistently find a deep hunger for appreciation. These people are not looking for financial reward and rarely desire high levels of praise. But they honestly express the need to be appreciated for their time and efforts. When appreciation is not forthcoming, they often become discouraged.

We have observed that within these organizations, there are often "encouragers"—those individuals who take it upon themselves to try to encourage staff and volunteers. These people are highly valued by others in the organization. However, the task is too much for a few random "encouragers" to successfully carry out. Often out of good intentions, they try to show appreciation to others in the way they themselves are encouraged. Thus, they often "miss the mark" and their efforts are not as successful as they wish. Implementing *Motivating by Appreciation* in church and ministry settings offers a practical tool to do what is desperately needed—expressing appreciation effectively.

MANUFACTURING FIRMS

We were told that the *Motivating by Appreciation* model would not work in the manufacturing sector. "This appreciation stuff is too 'touchy-feely,'" said one business consultant. Another business owner said, "Supervisors and line workers on the floor don't care about feelings. They just want to get the job done and get their paycheck."

However, what we found is that there are owners of manufacturing firms who understand the need to show appreciation to their team members, and who are actively looking for a model that will work within their organization. When the owner understands the potential benefits (review chapter 2, on the return on investment from appreciation and encouragement), and they find a practical model they can apply to their setting, they become visionary leaders and put the ideas to work within their company.

One such company, a small firm that manufactures and assembles electrical components, had us take their leadership team through the *Motivating by Appreciation* process. After first meeting together and giving an overview of the *MBA* model and the importance of appreciation in the workplace, the president, vice presidents, and directors of various areas took the **MBA Inventory**. We put together the leadership team's results from the inventory into a group chart so they could see what one another's primary, secondary, and lowest languages of appreciation were. Then, each leader put together an action plan of how they were going to communicate appreciation and encouragement to one another, starting by identifying one or two team members who would be their focus. A few weeks later, we had a follow-up meeting to report the potential positive results they were seeing, as well as discuss challenges they were encountering after they sought to implement the appreciation process.

It was fascinating to watch and hear the excitement and laughter in the room when the leadership team members reported their experiences. One director reported, "You know, it has been my experience over the years that when you communicate appreciation to your team, it creates a sense of loyalty. People will do almost anything for you because they know that you care about them personally. I think good managers understand this. But this model and the inventory gave me the specific information I need on *how* to encourage my people and what will be meaningful to them. Now I don't have to guess and wonder if I hit the mark. This is powerful stuff!"

We also explored the potential disconnect between the president's lowest language of appreciation (*Words of Affirmation*) and the primary language of two of his key leaders—which also was *Words of Affirmation.* The president said, "My primary language is *Acts of Service.* And to be totally honest, what that means to me is 'get 'er done.' You can help me best and encourage me by doing what you are supposed to do. That lightens my load. But I can see where, since I don't really value verbal praise, I have to work at communicating my appreciation more to you guys." At that point, one of his supervisees said in a good-natured tone of voice, "Ya think?" The room broke into a burst of laughter, including the president. This leadership team was learning that expressing appreciation can not only motivate, but can also be fun.

> **"You can help me best** *and encourage me* by **doing what you** **are supposed to do."**

OTHER POTENTIAL APPLICATIONS

We have just begun to scratch the surface of utilizing the appreciation model in all the various work settings. The need for encouragement and appreciation is also being communicated within **law enforcement** leadership circles. In his article in *Law and Order,* Robert Johnson argues that the ability to establish a personal connection with people separates effective leaders from mere administrators. He states, "While awards are nice, officers need the emotionally sincere expression of heartfelt approval and appreciation for a job well done. . . . When they sometimes make a questionable decision and they beat themselves up about it, they need encouragement, not judgment."[1]

We know that there is active interest in **government agencies.** These are work environments where there is little room for financial incentives or promotion based on one's performance. As consumers of services provided by these agencies, we often see the discouragement and apathy displayed by governmental employees. We firmly believe this is an area where the *MBA* model can significantly improve the work environment and daily experience of these individuals.

Research has already been done in **hotel** and **restaurant management** that demonstrates the need for the *MBA* model. More than three decades of research has shown that managers' style of leadership and behavior accounts for more than 70 percent of employees' perceptions of organizational climate. In fact, employees' feelings about management were found to be the main factor that improves employees' perceptions of their company's organizational climate. Successful managers develop and improve face-to-face communication with employees; they show care for and respect to employees by expressing appreciation and gratitude and encouraging and facilitating teamwork.[2]

Accountants are realizing the need within their profession to deal with the relational aspects within their job settings. In fact, the governing bodies of Certified Public Accountants have validated that emotional intelligence skills are critical to the success of the accounting profession. As a part of the training model for these skills, the "best practices" model for CPA firms includes the admonition to "encourage people to build a network of support and encouragement."[3]

As we discussed in chapter 2, a review of research shows that the role of appreciation and encouragement is being investigated in almost every work setting, from physicians and attorneys to teachers and childcare workers, from pastors and counselors to bus drivers and construction workers, even to baseball umpires and basketball referees!

The need for appreciation and encouragement is not limited to the United States or English-speaking nations. We have translated the **MBA Inventory** into Chinese, Spanish, and Vietnamese, and plan to pursue other languages as well (Turkish, Korean, German, and French).[4]

> *The need for appreciation and encouragement is not limited to the United States or English-speaking nations.*

We have already begun to utilize the *Motivating by Appreciation* model in a variety of international work settings and are finding managers and supervisors to be eagerly awaiting the availability of these resources. We are excited about the opportunities to help managers, supervisors, and coworkers in creating more positive work environments around the world.

MAKING IT PERSONAL

1. *From the following list, check the one that most closely identifies the organization or company with which you work.*

   - *Nonprofit organization*
   - *Financial services*
   - *Family-owned business*
   - *Schools*
   - *College or university*
   - *Medical/dental office*
   - *Other service business*
   - *Church*
   - *Large company*

   - *Health care provider*
   - *Manufacturing firm*
   - *Law enforcement*
   - *Government agency*
   - *Hotel*
   - *Restaurant*
   - *Retail outlet*
   - *Insurance office*
   - *Arts/media*

2. *In your work, what is your greatest challenge?*

3. *What is there about your work that gives you the deepest sense of satisfaction?*

4. *If you struggle to stay motivated on your job, what causes you the deepest sense of discouragement?*

5. *How do you think understanding the languages of appreciation could enhance your work environment?*

12

The Unique Characteristics of Volunteer Settings

Volunteering has been described as an activity in which time is given freely to benefit another person, group, or organization.[1] Over 50 percent of the adult population in the United States reports that they are involved in some volunteer activity over the course of a year. This indicates that tens of millions of individuals are giving of their time to serve others in some way. This is a huge workforce to be managed, as anyone who has been in charge of volunteers understands.

Volunteers include families, students, adolescents, young adults, couples, middle-aged adults, and senior adults. Many school-aged students begin volunteering as a part of their school activities, or through extracurricular organizations such as Girl Scouts, Boy Scouts, and church youth groups. However, many college-aged and young adults reduce their volunteering for a time, apparently while they are engaged in career development and pursuing significant personal relationships.

At any one point in time, 20 percent of adult females indicate they are volunteering. Interestingly, women report they become involved in volunteer activities to facilitate existing relationships with others, while men report they begin to volunteer to develop new relationships. Many adults become involved in volunteer activities for the express purpose of networking and developing business-related connections. This may occur through civic organizations such as Rotary International, the local Chamber of Commerce, or other nonprofit organizations.

While many believe that many senior adults who have retired from full-time work are a large part of the volunteer workforce, researchers have found that the number of people who begin to volunteer during retirement does not increase significantly. However, those who have been volunteering during their adult lives begin to contribute more of their time during their retirement.

WHERE VOLUNTEERS SERVE

In the United States and around the world, hundreds of thousands of organizations utilize volunteers every week. The breadth and span of their impact seems virtually immeasurable. Think for a moment about your weekly schedule and the number of organizations you interact with as a part of daily life. Many of these organizations have volunteers as a part of their workforce. Here is a list of some of the organizations who depend on volunteer help: schools (public and private), hospitals, libraries, sports teams, visitors' bureaus, airports, historical museums, zoos, animal shelters, boys and girls clubs, community festivals, art museums, churches and other places of worship, retirement communities, camps, music organizations, community service organizations, social service agencies, and environment-focused organizations.

Volunteers share their time and their talents. Volunteering may include spending time with others—being involved in big brother/big sister relationships or playing games with residents at a retirement community. But it may also involve using specific abilities such as administrative or clerical skills, musical or artistic talents, and other specialized professional skills (graphic design, carpentry, marketing). Many times volunteers are asked to provide physical labor to help lower the cost of a project.

Some volunteers make regular commitments—caring for shelter dogs in the afternoon, teaching a religious class for children, or working as a receptionist for a nonprofit organization. Other volunteers offer their time and services on a more sporadic schedule. For example, they may volunteer to help with a community's annual festival, drive students to debate events, or help to build a Habitat for Humanity house. Other individuals have personal traditions of helping a favorite organization by serving at one of their annual fund-raising events or organizational celebrations.

Understanding who these volunteers are, what they do, and how often they are engaged in serving is helpful information to those who are seeking to recruit and manage volunteers. Once they are recruited, volunteers can have a wide range of expectations of what they are willing to do and when and how often they are willing to serve. This leads to the challenge of keeping volunteers engaged and encouraged.

THE DOWNSIDE OF USING VOLUNTEERS

Organizations that utilize volunteers have an inherent dilemma. On one hand, volunteers are a valued resource. They provide services for "free" (in actuality, for the cost of training and supervising them). Therefore, organizations can leverage the use of volunteers to get a lot of work done that they otherwise could not financially afford. On the other hand, volunteers are typically not as reliable as paid employees. Since the working relationship between a volunteer and an organization is by nature informal, the reliability of volunteer staff is sometimes less than desirable.

Volunteers can be demanding—expecting certain things from the organization and unwilling to do certain jobs. Volunteers may become upset or offended by something they observe in the organization. They may, in this state of mind, create turmoil or simply discontinue their volunteer service.

The truth is that sometimes volunteers are more costly to the organization than the value of the work they complete. The cost of lost time by the paid staff to oversee, house, feed, and entertain large groups of volunteers can be huge. This reality has led some companies to rethink the cost-effectiveness of using volunteers.

But the biggest challenge that most supervisors of volunteers have is the fact that volunteers tend to be "short term." While many individuals are involved in volunteer service, being committed over time to the same organization is less common. Many volunteers work for an organization for a few weeks or months, then fade away and discontinue their service. The turnover rate of volunteer workers is extremely high and is one of the major challenges for administrators of organizations that utilize volunteers.

UNDERSTANDING THE IMPORTANCE OF JOB SATISFACTION FOR VOLUNTEERS

Job satisfaction is not an issue relegated solely to for-profit businesses. Those individuals who work for not-for-profit organizations and those who volunteer also desire a sense of satisfaction from the work they perform. Researchers have investigated the impact

*Retention of volunteers is **one of the key challenges** for nonprofit organizations.*

of job satisfaction in these not-for-profit organizations and on the volunteers who work for them. Retention of volunteers is one of the key challenges for nonprofit organizations. Some of the research findings include:

Low job satisfaction increases job turnover. When employees and volunteers in nonprofit organizations do not like their jobs or the characteristics of the organization they're working with, they are more likely to quit. They may, in fact, move to a different organization or a different type of work, but they are not likely to continue in a position that does not bring personal satisfaction.

Turnover affects the quality of services delivered. When organizations have high turnover, it directly affects their ability to provide consistent, quality services to those they serve. High turnover makes it hard for organizations to adequately train new volunteers, and their lack of experience can affect the quality of services provided.

Volunteers are more likely to quit because their efforts go unrecognized. When volunteers feel that no one notices or appreciates their efforts, they become discouraged and quit relatively quickly. A sense of lack of recognition and appreciation is a significant factor in why volunteers quit.

One of the "best practices" nonprofits can follow includes volunteer recognition and appreciation. Professionals who consult regularly with volunteer-based organizations to help them improve their effectiveness have found that communicating appreciation is core to becoming successful in accomplishing organizational goals.

Many volunteers report the main reason they quit is a sense of isolation and lack of support from others. Volunteers need to feel connected with and supported by their supervisors and coworkers. Otherwise, their duration of service will be limited.

WHY PEOPLE START VOLUNTEERING, AND WHY THEY CONTINUE

As a psychologist, I (Paul) often deal with problem behaviors in people's lives. Individuals may seek help in dealing with anger issues, depression, a desire to lose weight, or to improve their marriage—the list of behaviors is almost endless. When it comes to behavior change, there is a fundamental principle that must be understood: The reasons why a person starts a behavior and the reasons why the behavior continues are often very different.

This is important to understand for volunteers because the reasons people initially begin to volunteer are often different than why they continue as a volunteer. Let's explore this by first examining common reasons people start volunteering:

- Such service has been part of their family's values and lifestyle while growing up.
- It is a requirement for an organization of which they are a member.

- To socialize with existing friends.
- To develop new social contacts.
- To give back to an organization that has served them or their family.
- In response to a specific need or crisis (flood, tornado, hurricane, etc.).
- Out of concern for a need highlighted in the community.
- From religious beliefs and motives of helping those less fortunate.
- From a personal desire to share with others the blessings they have experienced.

Note that "recognition" is not among the reasons people volunteer.

But why do people continue to volunteer? Commonly cited reasons include:

- Experiencing a sense of contribution to a cause greater than myself.
- Being able to make a difference in one's life or in my community.
- Enjoying the social relationships developed while working together on helpful projects.
- Receiving positive feedback regarding the service I provide.
- Having a sense of loyalty or commitment toward the organization or cause.

Keeping volunteers engaged over time is a major challenge for nonprofit managers. Thus, we believe that understanding the needs and desires of volunteer workers is key to being able to keep them volunteering over longer periods of time. If you analyze the reasons that people continue to volunteer, they fall into two categories: social connectedness and perceived impact.

When volunteers feel connected to others—those they are serving, their coworkers, and the staff of the organization—the longevity of their commitment increases dramatically. Conversely, we know that when volunteers feel isolated from others, when they don't feel supported by staff members, and when they don't feel relationally connected to those they are serving, they will quit.

> *Volunteers need input and perspective from their supervisors in order to understand the impact they are truly having.*

Most volunteers also want to "make a difference." They want to know that what they are doing is important and is having a positive impact on others. The problem is, many volunteer efforts do not make significant and visible differences immediately. Therefore, volunteers can't always see the impact of their service. It is critical for their supervisors and support staff to help them see how what they are doing fits into the big picture, and how it will make a difference over time. Volunteers need input and perspective from their supervisors in order to understand the impact they are truly having.

HOW APPRECIATION MAKES A DIFFERENCE

In bolstering volunteers' sense of both social connectedness and perceived impact, the role of the supervisor and the encouragement of colleagues are exceedingly important. Effectively conveying your appreciation for the work they are doing in ways that are meaningful to the volunteer can significantly boost volunteer retention.

We have found that organizations that take the time to find

out how their volunteers are best encouraged and that discover their primary languages of appreciation (through using the **MBA Inventory**) have far more success in "hitting the target" with their volunteers. Supervisors also have communicated that they are amazed at how much less time and energy it takes to encourage volunteers when they know what will encourage that person, versus putting on large appreciation events that miss the mark for many of their workers.

If you are an administrator of a nonprofit organization or a supervisor of volunteers, consider this: Wouldn't it be helpful to write notes and give verbal thanks to those individuals for whom it really matters? Wouldn't it be delightful to give a small number of gifts to those who appreciate them, and to know what gift they would like? Think of the amount of time and energy you could save if you spent time individually or in small groups with those who value quality time. Wouldn't it reduce your anxiety to know which volunteers value and are motivated by working together and which are fine with working independently?

One of the most common complaints by volunteers about attempted displays of appreciation is that it feels like "one size fits all." Our internal research shows that public recognition is one of the least favorite forms of receiving appreciation. Yet this is a favorite practice of nonprofit administrators when they give the "volunteer of the year" award or have the chairperson of the fund-raising event stand up and receive recognition. We believe that when administrators understand the languages of appreciation, they will be able to be far more effective in their efforts to express appreciation to their volunteers. (Please see "How to Reward Volunteers" in the Appreciation Toolkit at the back of the book or at appreciation.com/resources.)

Laura is the director of a social service agency that recruits volunteers to mentor high school girls who are pregnant or have an infant. The goal of the mentors is to help keep the girls in school and graduate, provide emotional support during their pregnancy, and give practical training to them as a young mother. It is a high risk/high impact relationship.

When we started working with Laura, she reported her greatest need was to answer the question, "How do I encourage and support my volunteers so they don't become discouraged and quit?" Her mentors are the "engine" of the services the organization provides. Without them the whole train stops. When she found out about the **MBA Inventory** and the coaching model we were developing, she couldn't wait to start. In fact, she had us attend the next meeting with her volunteers where we introduced the concepts of encouragement and appreciation (many of them were already familiar with *The 5 Love Languages*). Then each volunteer took the **MBA Inventory**.

Two weeks later, we discussed their inventory results and presented the volunteers a group chart that indicated the primary, secondary, and least important language of appreciation for each volunteer. They were excited to know how to encourage one another and started making plans to do so.

A few weeks later, we followed up with Laura. She was glowing with the positive effect the new initiatives were having on her team. She indicated morale among the mentors was up and her relationships with her team members had significantly improved.

We believe Laura's story will be experienced in any volunteer-driven organization that will take the time to help workers and staff discover each other's primary language of appreciation. Because we know that volunteers continue to be motivated when they receive expressions of appreciation and thus feel connected to colleagues and staff, we strongly urge administrators in organizations that rely heavily on volunteer help to utilize the insights of *Motivating by Appreciation*.

MAKING IT PERSONAL

Volunteers

1. *If you are a volunteer, on a scale of 0–10, how much appreciation do you feel coming from your supervisor? What might your supervisor do that would raise the level of your sense of appreciation?*

2. *Do you work closely with other volunteers? If so, list the names of those with whom you work most closely and rank your sense of appreciation from those individuals on a scale of 0–10. What might each of these fellow volunteers do or say that would increase your sense of appreciation?*

3. *When is the last time you expressed appreciation to your supervisor for his/her role in your volunteer work? What did you do to express appreciation? How well do you think your supervisor received your expression of appreciation?*

4. *When is the last time you expressed appreciation to one of your volunteer colleagues? How did you express this appreciation and how did they respond?*

5. *Do you know your own primary language of appreciation? If your answer is no, consider taking the **MBA Inventory**.*

6. Do you know the primary language of appreciation of your supervisor and your fellow volunteers? If your answer is no, perhaps you could encourage your colleagues to take the **MBA Inventory**. You may also wish to give a copy of this book to your supervisor.

Administrators and Managers

1. If you manage or supervise volunteers, what has been your greatest challenge?

2. What is your organization currently doing to express appreciation to volunteers? Do you have a method of receiving feedback from volunteers on their level of satisfaction in the volunteer work they are doing?

3. Since feeling genuine appreciation is such a significant factor in job satisfaction, perhaps you would like to encourage your volunteers to take the **MBA Inventory** so that you and they could understand each other's primary language of appreciation.

4. Do you feel that you are adequately communicating the importance of the role that volunteers are playing in reaching the overall objective of your organization? What might you do to enhance their sense that they are "making a difference" by what they are doing?

5. Do you sense that your volunteers feel socially connected with their coworkers, those whom they are serving, and the staff of the organization? What might you do to strengthen the social connectedness of your volunteers?

Overcoming Common Obstacles

13

Does a Person's Language of Appreciation Change over Time?

W hen we work with companies on applying the *Motivating by Appreciation* model, we're often asked, "Does a person's primary language of appreciation change in certain situations?" If the answer to that question is yes, then a second question arises: "How do we know if a person's primary appreciation language has changed?" The answer to those questions is the focus of this chapter.

We want to begin by saying that we believe one's primary appreciation language tends to stay the primary language throughout a lifetime. It is like many other personality traits. A person who is highly organized will always be an organizer. On the other hand, there is the person who will seemingly spend half a lifetime looking for their phone. A morning person will always find their most productive hours before 11 a.m. while the night person will come alive after 10 p.m. These traits tend to persist for a lifetime. They are a part of who we are.

Having said that, we want to clarify that we are not suggesting that people do not change over time. We know that a disorganized personality can take positive steps in becoming more organized. A night person with the help of a little caffeine may not see the sunrise—but they may get up in time to hear the birds sing.

And even though a primary language of appreciation may be a lifetime trait in a person, there are certain factors and seasons of life when one's secondary language of appreciation may ascend the ladder of importance and one's primary language may, for the moment, tend to decrease in emotional value. There may also be situations in which one's least important language may become meaningful. We want to discuss two situations in which one's primary language of appreciation may tend to shift in importance.

LIFE STAGES AND LIFE CIRCUMSTANCES

First, one's current life stage and life circumstances can have an impact. Many of us have either experienced personally or worked with colleagues who have had a family member struggle with significant medical problems. A spouse or child may have been in a serious accident or have life-threatening health issues that result in a prolonged hospitalization and period of recovery. During these times, we are all "stretched to the max," burdened with demands on our time and emotions. We worry about the unknown—what will happen to our loved one?

Emotional support and encouragement are critical during these times, from family and friends and from colleagues at work. During these intense times of life, our language of appreciation may shift.

For example, Michael is a hardworking accountant in a large accounting firm. When he first took the **MBA Inventory**, his primary language of appreciation was identified as *Words of Affirmation*. Michael agreed with this assessment. What really made him feel appreciated was when people recognized his work and verbally affirmed him.

Six months after Michael took the inventory, his wife was diagnosed with cancer. The next two years involved frequent trips to the doctor, two surgeries, and chemotherapy. During this time, Michael's colleagues at work gathered around and strongly supported him. Two female coworkers would stay with Michael's children so he could accompany his wife to her medical appointments. Two other employees arranged to take meals to Michael's home after each of his wife's surgeries.

Michael later said to these four coworkers, "I will never forget what you have done for me. I could not have made it without your help." To this day, he looks back on that experience as one of the times when he felt most deeply appreciated by his colleagues. During that season of Michael's life, the language of *Acts of Service* spoke more deeply to him emotionally than *Words of Affirmation*. When we looked at his **MBA Inventory**, we noted that *Acts of Service* was his secondary language of appreciation. But during this intensely personal crisis, his secondary language became his primary language.

"Action steps" within one's favored appreciation language also may shift with different stages of life. Bryan is a sales manager for a manufacturing firm. In his midthirties, he frequently travels to see potential customers and as part of doing business goes out to dinner at fairly nice restaurants with his customers. Earlier in his adult life, like many young couples, Bryan and his wife, Sandi, lived on a pretty tight budget, so eating out was a rare treat. At that point in his career, Bryan and Sandi would have welcomed a gift certificate to a nice restaurant as a demonstration of appreciation for his good work. However, at this stage a gift card to a restaurant would have less value to Bryan, even though his primary appreciation language is *Tangible Gifts*. Now, since he and Sandi have developed an interest in music, they prefer concert tickets. This is an example of how the specific action step within a language may change over time and in various life stages.

Or consider Brenda, a top performer in a national sales organization. Her primary language of appreciation is *Words of Affirmation*. When she received her first public recognition as "salesperson of the month," she called her mother and told her about her success. She even read the words on the award that she received. She felt genuinely affirmed and appreciated. Four years later, Brenda's closet is filled with awards and plaques that she has received for various accomplishments. She now takes it all in stride and seldom shares the award with her mother or anyone else. She simply puts the plaque in the closet and moves on to her next accomplishment.

Recently her supervisor stopped by her office and said, "Brenda, I have given you more plaques and awards than anyone in the history of the company. I could give you another plaque if you like. But I wanted to stop by personally and let you know how much I appreciate your contribution to the company. Not only are you a great salesperson, but you also motivate others. In many ways, you are the most significant person in our sales force. I want you to know that I sincerely value your contribution to the company. Next week, if you don't object, I'll give you another plaque. But I just wanted you to know that, with me, it's not just the perfunctory giving of an award, but I sincerely appreciate what you are doing." Brenda thanked her supervisor for his comments. When he left the office, tears came to her eyes and she said to herself, "I believe he really does appreciate my efforts."

While *Words of Affirmation* is Brenda's primary appreciation language, it was the fact that her supervisor took the time to come by her office and verbally express his appreciation that spoke deeply to her. This was more effective than the public recognition in front of her colleagues. Her supervisor spoke both the language of *Quality Time* and *Words of Affirmation*.

So how do you know when a person's primary language of appreciation may have changed for a season or that their action steps have shifted in importance? Sometimes you can observe it by simply acknowledging their present circumstances. Michael's colleagues were aware of his wife's illness, and those closest to him knew what would help and responded instinctively. They were not thinking, "What is Mike's appreciation language?" They were thinking, "What could we do that would be helpful in this situation?" But in so responding, they communicated appreciation to Michael in the deepest possible way. Sometimes if we are simply in tune with our colleague's life circumstances, we will be able to intuitively know what help would mean the most.

On the other hand, Bryan's supervisor or colleagues may not have known that a gift certificate to a nice restaurant was no longer as meaningful to him as it had been earlier in his life. The fact that Bryan preferred a ticket to a concert rather than a gift certificate to a restaurant would have to be communicated to his supervisor and colleagues. That is why we encourage those who take the **MBA Inventory** and list their "action steps" to revisit these action steps semiannually and provide new information as to ways that might make them feel appreciated. If this can be worked into a semiannual review by the supervisor, it makes it much easier for the employee.

Brenda's supervisor may not have known that his visit to her office and the extended time he gave her would be so meaningful in terms of communicating his appreciation. However, if Brenda shares how meaningful his visit and words were, the supervisor will now know that *Quality Time* with *Words of Affirmation* are more meaningful than mere public recognition.

TONYA, GLENN, AND INTERPERSONAL DYNAMICS

Allow us to think like psychologists for just a moment. In the early days of psychology (from the early 1900s through the 1970s), the focus of psychotherapists was primarily on individuals—their personality characteristics, behavior patterns, habits, and how they thought. However, eventually psychologists became aware that an individual's behavior occurred within a context—within a system (of relationships) rather than in isolation. This led to the development of what is called Systems Theory. The basic idea is that people's behaviors and thoughts are best understood if you understand the system in which they live. This discovery led to the development of marriage and family therapy and social psychology. It sought to give a more thorough understanding of how one's social context (the people with whom they interact) changes how a person behaves. An obvious example is how a teenager greets her friends versus how she greets her grandmother.

The key point of this discussion for our purposes is that a person's primary language of appreciation may shift, depending on the person to whom they are relating. For example, what they desire from a colleague may differ somewhat from what they desire from a supervisor. The personality of the supervisor may also affect what the employee would like to receive as an expression of appreciation. In exploring this issue, it is evident that our languages of appreciation, while residing primarily in "who we are," are also influenced by the characteristics of the person with whom we are interacting. An easy example of this is to think of how you interact with your current supervisor and compare that with how you interacted with your previous supervisors. You are essentially the same person (although you have probably changed some), but you communicate and respond differently, depending on the personal characteristics of the supervisor.

This interpersonal dynamic impacts our language of appreciation as well. Consider this example. Tonya generally values compliments and other verbal expressions of appreciation; this is her primary appreciation language. However, Tonya's current supervisor is a high-energy, extremely verbal marketing professional. Glenn is a dynamic individual who showers positive verbal comments on virtually everyone he meets. "What a great day! How is it going, Joseph? I sure appreciate the work you got done for me yesterday. You did a super job!" And on he goes to the next team member.

People love Glenn because he is so positive and encouraging. However, because he offers so much verbal praise, it can somewhat diminish its perceived value by those close to him. So when Glenn compliments Tonya, she is grateful but also tends to discount the message somewhat.

What really makes an impact on Tonya is when Glenn stops by her office and asks not only how things are going but also what suggestions she has that might enhance the performance of the department. When he stops long enough to have a conversation with her, she senses that he sincerely appreciates her efforts and insights. She knows that Glenn is fast-paced and always on the go. He rarely sits still for extended conversations. He is often interrupted by phone calls, text messages, or people wanting to talk with him. To his credit, he responds quickly to those who are contacting him, but Glenn can also be rather distracted. In the middle of a conversation, he can think of someone he needs to call and does so immediately. "Hold that thought," he may say. "I need to call Kevin about something real quick. It will only take a second." Thus, when he takes time to not only verbally affirm Tonya but also listen to her ideas, she senses his sincerity.

Interestingly, *Quality Time* is Tonya's secondary language of appreciation. But in relationship with Glenn, it clearly becomes more important than her primary appreciation language. Therefore, although her **MBA Inventory** results would communicate to Glenn that Tonya values verbal affirmation, in actuality her primary way of receiving encouragement from Glenn is to have a quality conversation in which he gives her his undivided attention.

Who is going to know this shift in languages? Tonya. Over time, if she pays attention to her internal responses, she will become aware that what she really desires from her supervisor is *Quality Time*. So, it will be important for her to clarify this both for herself and to Glenn. She might have the following conversation.

"Glenn, can I have a minute? I need to share something with you. You know how we all took that inventory on appreciation so you could find out how best to encourage us in ways that are meaningful to each of us? You probably remember that my primary language is verbal affirmation. I love to be complimented and hear how well I'm doing, and you are great at that. But what I have realized is, since you are so complimentary and encouraging to everyone and since you are so busy, what I really value are those times when you stop by my office, ask me how I'm doing, and ask for my suggestions on how we can improve the efficiency of the company. Don't get me wrong. I still want to hear what you like about what I'm doing. But even more meaningful to me is the sense that you genuinely care about my ideas on what we can do to enhance the efficiency of the company. Does that make sense?"

> When a person receives an adequate supply of their primary language of appreciation, **their secondary language may then become more important.**

Glenn now has the information he needs to effectively communicate appreciation to Tonya. Because of the personal dynamics, Tonya's primary language from Glenn has shifted from *Words of Affirmation* to *Quality Time*. However, in Tonya's relationship to her colleagues, her primary language of appreciation continues to be words of affirmation.

There is one other factor that is illustrated by Tonya's experience. When a person receives an adequate supply of their primary language of appreciation, their secondary language may then become more important. Tonya's primary language of appreciation is *Words of Affirmation*. That's who she is. But inasmuch as Glenn gave an abundance of words of affirmation, it had become less meaningful, and *Quality Time* became more meaningful. Our guess is that if Glenn stopped giving her verbal affirmation on a regular basis, her primary language of appreciation would quickly revert to *Words of Affirmation*.

Or consider Tim's situation. He is a hard worker, with high expectations of himself. However, because of the nature of his job and the fact that the company has downsized, he sometimes becomes overwhelmed with the quantity of work expected of him. On the **MBA Inventory**, his primary language of appreciation was *Acts of Service*. When colleagues pitch in and help him with a project, he genuinely feels appreciated. And yet Tim has one colleague whose help he does not appreciate. This colleague is an incessant talker, while Tim is a rather quiet person. When the colleague is helping him, he is talking and joking and telling stories constantly. Tim finds this very distracting and annoying. He cannot give his attention to his own work while his colleague is attempting to help him. Therefore, because of the personal dynamics in their relationship, Tim's primary language with this colleague is not *Acts of Service*. If this colleague offers to help him, he will now say, "No thank you. I've got it covered. Thanks for asking."

We hope these illustrations help clarify the impact of personal dynamics on one's language of appreciation. The remaining question is, "How would Tim's talkative colleague know that *Acts of Service* is not the primary appreciation language that Tim would like to receive from him?" After all, he may have seen Tim's **MBA Inventory** printout and be sincere in his efforts to express appreciation by offering to help. Our suggestion is: Before speaking what you think is the person's primary language, ask, "Would this be helpful to you?" If their response is, "No thank you. I've got it covered," and you get this response at least twice, then you can assume that their primary language of appreciation *from you* is not *Acts of Service*.

This straightforward inquiry can be used with all of the languages of appreciation. If your perception is that a person's primary language of appreciation is *Words of Affirmation*, you might ask, "If I wanted to express my appreciation to you, would words of affirmation be the best way to do it?" If the answer is yes, then give your speech of affirmation. If they suggest something else, then remember: They are the expert on themselves. Let their answer guide you in knowing how to express appreciation to them. If you perceive that *Receiving Tangible Gifts* is their primary language of appreciation, you might say, "When I was in Dallas, I bought you a little gift because I wanted you to know how much I appreciate what you do for the company. But if gifts is not your language of appreciation, I'd be glad to give it to someone else. Would you like to have it?" Because you have asked, even if their primary language

> Remember: **They are the expert** on themselves. Let their answer guide you in knowing **how to express appreciation** to them.

is not *Receiving Gifts*, they would probably accept it as a genuine expression of your appreciation. The very process of asking, "Would this be meaningful?" tends to communicate sincerity.

The point we are trying to make in this chapter is that you should not be surprised if you discover that your primary language of appreciation shifts in certain circumstances and with certain people. Nor should you be surprised to discover that the same may be true of your colleagues. This does not mean that the concept of having primary, secondary, and lower languages of appreciation is invalid. Rather it is an acceptance of the fluidity of life and that we are human beings, not unchanging machines.

We encourage you to be aware of your own internal reactions and the responses of your colleagues. Life is not static; people and their lives change over time. We believe the best managers are those who know their people well, continue to get to know them, and make appropriate changes as needed. The reality of the factors we have discussed in this chapter again point to the importance of having regular evaluation sessions with employees. As a part of these proactive evaluations, you can easily discover any changes in their primary and secondary languages of appreciation or the action steps that they would prefer.

HOW DO PERSONAL "LOVE LANGUAGES" RELATE TO THE LANGUAGES OF APPRECIATION?

For those individuals who are familiar with *The 5 Love Languages* and have gone through the process of identifying their own preferred love language in personal relationships, they often are intrigued about the relationship between the two sets of languages (go to www.5lovelanguages.com for more information on these books). We are frequently asked, "What is the relationship between a person's personal love languages and their languages of appreciation? Are they identical? Are they somewhat related? Or are they totally different?"

First, for those who are not familiar directly with *The 5 Love Languages*, let us provide some context. I (Gary) found in working with couples (often in the context of marriage counseling) that the husband and wife often had different ways that they communicated love with each other. After gathering data for several years, I found that these expressions of affection fell into five broad categories or languages. The results of my research and the practical implications for marital relationships are explained in the original *5 Love Languages*. We then discovered that these personal languages of love and affection applied to other relationships as well, so we investigated this issue further and wrote *5 Love Languages of Children* (coauthored with Ross Campbell, MD), *5 Love Languages of Teens*, and for single adults, *5 Love Languages, Singles Edition*. The response has been overwhelming over the past nineteen years, with over six million copies of some form of the love language book being sold in over forty languages. The foundational concepts were then applied to restoring relationships in *The 5 Languages of Apology*, coauthored with Jennifer Thomas.

*How do a person's preferred languages of love **in personal friendships and family relationships** compare to their preferred languages of **appreciation in the workplace?***

The question then is, "How do a person's preferred languages of love in personal friendships and family relationships compare to their preferred languages of appreciation in the workplace?" We have three different sources of information to help answer this question: first, from a theoretical perspective on the nature of human behavior; second, from our professional experience in working with the five languages over the years; and finally, from information we have gathered from clients and trainees, and some beginning research data.

Research on human behavior has found two fairly common and consistent themes: (a) people generally behave the same over time unless there is a major life-changing event that affects them; and (b) individuals' specific actions do vary across settings and especially in response to those with whom they are interacting. The whole concept of "personality" is built upon the belief that individuals have common patterns of behaving and relating to others—to the point that these patterns are predictable and become character qualities of the person. But we also know that people's actions can vary significantly depending on whom they are relating to—their spouse, their child, their boss, a friend, or their mother.

We can say, then, that in general the ways people experience and prefer acts of encouragement, appreciation, or affection would be similar over time and many settings. But we would also predict that there is a good chance for many people that how they relate to others, and how they prefer others communicate appreciation to them, would change in response to who the other person is and the type of relationship they have.

The second source of understanding the relationship between personal love languages and languages of appreciation in the workplace comes from the years of experience we have had in working with these concepts. Clearly, one of us (Gary) has more experience in the context of the love languages within personal relationships, while the other (Paul) has had more focus on work-based relationships and the languages of appreciation. We both independently came to the same conclusion: that over time we would find out that there is a moderate correlation and overlap between individuals' preferred languages, regardless of the setting or type of relationship. But we also expect that there would not be an exact overlay, and there will be variation both across most preferred and least preferred languages. This is, in fact, what we have found.

Clients and individuals who have gone through training sessions with us consistently report that they believe that, for themselves, there is a general overlap across their languages of appreciation in the workplace and their personal love languages, but it is not 100 percent. For example, Betsy, a lead teacher in a middle school, stated, "Receiving verbal praise is important to me in either setting. So it is one of my top two languages on both scales. But quality time with my husband is far more important and comes out higher on the five love languages scale."

Similarly, Chris, the comptroller for a corporation, stated, "I think I am basically the same person whether I am at work or at home, but clearly there are expressions of affection I value from my wife that I don't look for from my colleagues at work. So I would expect my preferred languages to differ in those two relationships." On the other hand, many people say that their primary languages of love and appreciation are the same but that the secondary languages change depending on the setting.

In a study with adjunct faculty at a university, we found that only 38 percent of the participants had the same primary language on both the **MBA Inventory** and the five love languages profile. *So for the majority of this group, their primary languages weren't the same.* However, when looking at the results more closely, we found the following: Sixty-nine percent of the faculty members had their primary love language as either their first or second highest language of appreciation. That is, if *Quality Time* was their highest love language, then *Quality Time* was either their first or second preferred language of appreciation. And the results were essentially the same when going the other direction. If verbal praise was an individual's highest language of appreciation, then 67 percent of the time *Words of Affirmation* was either their first or second highest love language. These results confirmed both what we believed and the self-perceptions workers were reporting to us.

We can conclude by saying that it is reasonable to expect that an individual's preferred language of appreciation may vary significantly over time in response to different life events, life stages, and the individuals with whom they are interacting. Similarly, most people will have some commonalities in their preferred languages in personal relationships and work-based relationships, but frequently there will be differences across the relational settings.

MAKING IT PERSONAL

1. *Can you remember circumstances in your own life when your primary language of appreciation seemed to shift? What were the circumstances that stimulated this shift?*

2. *If you have experienced a painful personal event in your life, how did your colleagues support you during that time? Did you find their support to be meaningful?*

3. *If you have seen a shift in your primary language of appreciation or the action steps you would like to receive from others, have you communicated this information to those with whom you work?*

4. *Can you identify personal dynamics between you and a colleague that lead you to be nonreceptive to their expressions of appreciation?*

5. *When you compare your present supervisor with a former supervisor, do you see a difference in the language of appreciation that you desired from each of them? Why do you think this is true?*

14

Overcoming Your Challenges

The question is not, "Do you appreciate your coworkers or those who work under your direction?" The real question is, "Do they *feel* appreciated?" Our experience has led us to the conclusion that there are thousands of people who work in what they consider to be a "thankless environment." In many cases their managers and colleagues are unaware of these feelings. They observe that the employee does his or her job in a satisfactory manner, and that is all that they expect. However, the employee works with little enthusiasm and is likely performing far below his potential.

If communicating appreciation and encouragement to those we work with was easy, then everyone in the company would be a happy camper. There would be no need for this book or for a structured approach to motivating by appreciation. The truth is, there are challenges that get in the way of effectively

197

expressing gratitude to our colleagues. Some are internal issues—attitudes, thoughts, and beliefs. Other challenges are external and relate to corporate structures and procedures.

These challenges need to be faced realistically, but they can be overcome. Here are some of the common challenges and our suggestions on how to solve them as you seek to create a positive work climate.

CHALLENGE #1: BUSYNESS

In the work we have done with organizations, the absolute number one most frequent reason that appreciation is not a regu-lar part of communication is the *busyness of the team members.* This can be true of managers, individual team members, or those who work with volunteer organizations. Almost everyone feels stretched in their daily responsibilities. Who is sitting around trying to figure out what to do with all of their extra time? Not many of the people we have met. Why is this? At least part of the answer seems to lie in one of the following areas: (a) having no margin in one's day to allow for interruptions, problems, or unforeseen challenges; (b) high and often unrealistic expectations by managers, customers, or the workers themselves; and (c) financial pressures in the global economy today.

Regardless of the source of busyness, this issue is a major obstacle to overcome if managers and colleagues are going to successfully implement the principles of motivating by appreciation. Workers must have the mental space to observe others if they are going to appreciate what they are doing. They also must possess the emotional energy to consider and plan the best way to express appreciation to a particular colleague. Without available mental, physical, and emotional space, nothing will change.

Overcoming Busyness

The most important way to overcome busyness is to prioritize. Some things *are* more important than others. If the most important things do not take priority, then our time and energy invested in other matters will fail to produce the desired results.

We highly recommend Steven Covey's excellent books *First Things First*[1] and *The Seven Habits of Highly Effective People.*[2] These books provide a helpful process to aid leaders and team members identify those priorities that are most important to them and make them a part of their daily and weekly routine. If our priorities are not reflected in our schedule, then they cease to be priorities. Covey's quadrant of priorities—important/not important, urgent/not urgent—has been helpful to each of us in our personal and professional lives.

We believe that for supervisors, business owners, and managers, giving time and energy to show appreciation to your colleagues and those who work for you is an important task that will yield large dividends in your organization and the services you provide. However, for many managers, expressing appreciation is usually not urgent, and if you do not intentionally plan to do it, the nonimportant but seemingly urgent matters of the day can crowd out the daily discipline of communicating appreciation to your team.

CHALLENGE #2: THE BELIEF THAT COMMUNICATING APPRECIATION IS NOT IMPORTANT FOR YOUR ORGANIZATION

Some organizational leaders hear about the languages of appreciation and the motivating by appreciation concept and immediately say, "I can see how that would be good in some companies, but it won't work in my industry. Construction workers aren't big into saying thanks or caring about how others feel." We have heard similar comments from a variety of business leaders in the areas of finance, sales organizations, Fortune 500 corporations, restaurant chains, auto repair shops, and various other work settings. Interestingly, the results of research paint a different picture. Almost all research indicates the positive impact of nonfinancial rewards on the lives of workers in almost every industry.

What we have found is that the type of business or organization is not an important factor. The real issue is the mind-set of the owner, director, or supervisor. If leadership does not feel that appreciation is important, they are not likely to see the need for expressing appreciation to those who work for them. If this mind-set is not changed, then their employees are forced to live in a thankless community, wishing that things could be better.

Overcoming the Attitude "Appreciation Is Not Important for My Organization"

We have found that in reality, the *Motivating by Appreciation* model can be successfully utilized in virtually any organizational setting, regardless of how hard-nosed or financially driven the culture may be. The most important variable is that a leader or supervisor understands the power of individuals feeling valued for the work they do and the contributions they make toward the organization's success.

For each leader who has reacted negatively, we have had other leaders in the same industries who recognized almost immediately the value of employees feeling appreciated. When they hear of the **MBA Inventory** and the concept of individualizing expressions of appreciation, they are eager to get started. We have seen leaders in traditionally "tough men" industries (manufacturing, commercial construction, and residential building) who have chosen to include appreciation as a part of the company's culture. The results have been high loyalty from employees, low turnover rates, and higher ratings of job satisfaction. These characteristics help make the company financially profitable.

One corporate executive changed his mind. The first time he heard about the concept, he said, "I don't really care about how my people feel about their work. They are driven individuals who are motivated by potential financial success, and we set up a system to reward them in that way." Later, after the global financial meltdown, he came back to us, saying, "If there is a way to encourage and motivate our employees without paying them more, I'm all for it. How can we get started?"

In a world where employees are often expected to do more work for less pay, learning to express meaningful appreciation may make the difference between failure and success for the company.

CHALLENGE #3: FEELING OVERWHELMED
WITH EXISTING RESPONSIBILITIES

When working with the volunteer staff of a nonprofit organization, one of the team members blurted out in distress, "I'm all for this appreciation stuff and I think it is a great idea. But just thinking about keeping track of my teams' languages of appreciation and their action steps overwhelms me. It is all I can do to keep up with my current responsibilities." Her openness and candor was important to us, and we expressed understanding.

Feeling overwhelmed is more than being busy; it also includes the sense of weighty responsibility. Some individuals, either in temporary circumstances or in longer lifestyle patterns, can easily feel overloaded. They feel that expressing appreciation to coworkers is just another responsibility added to their plate. If pressured to participate in the process of taking the **MBA Inventory** and to think seriously about learning to express appreciation in meaningful ways, this person can become very negative and disgruntled. That is why we always encourage companies to let participation in the *MBA* be done on a voluntary basis.

> *Feeling overwhelmed is* **more than being busy**; *it also includes* **the sense of weighty responsibility.**

Overcoming Team Members Feeling Overwhelmed

This is going to sound awfully "psychologist-like," but the first and best response you can give to a team member who is feeling overwhelmed is to acknowledge and validate their perspective. Do your best therapist imitation and say, "Boy, it sounds like you are really feeling overwhelmed." Then listen with concern as they expound further on their feelings.

On the other hand, telling them, "Oh, come on. It's not that big of a deal. We are just asking you to do what you are already doing," generally doesn't make things better. Ignoring their sense of exasperation and moving on with the plan usually leads to resistance or resentment. In some situations, after venting their feelings, and feeling heard by their manager, some employees say, "It really isn't that big of a deal; I can do this. I guess I just needed to vent. I really do want my coworkers to feel appreciated." In other situations, the person is reacting to what they think they heard, not really what you attempted to say. So, follow up and clarify by saying, "Let me make sure you are clear on what I am asking and not asking you to do." This process of clarification can reduce resistance.

However, other members may need you to give them the option to not pursue this plan at this time. As noted above, in working with organizations, we propose that participation in the process should be voluntary and not a top-down directive. This strengthens the impact of the actions individuals choose to take to encourage others. Their efforts to validate coworkers are not seen as something they were "supposed to do." An employee who chooses not to participate in the **MBA Inventory** today may well choose to get involved two months later. We are not trying to force people to do something they do not wish to do. We are trying to help those who sincerely would like to express appreciation and encouragement to coworkers in a more effective manner.

> *An employee who chooses* **not to participate** *in the* **MBA Inventory** *today may well choose to* **get involved** **two months later.**

CHALLENGE #4: STRUCTURAL AND PROCEDURAL ISSUES THAT INHIBIT EFFECTIVE PATTERNS OF COMMUNICATION

When working with one office team, we were following up with encouraging emails to the team members. One of the staff responded to an email by saying, "I am trying to encourage Jenna but I just haven't seen her this week. We are working different shifts with little overlap of time, and when we are together we are generally working in different areas. So I don't have much opportunity for interaction with her."

Sometimes there are logistical issues that interfere with the process of sharing appreciation for others. Varying schedules, few natural opportunities for interaction, working on different projects, and nonmatching vacations often make it difficult to express appreciation to certain coworkers.

There can also be structural challenges to overcome. Those who work in larger corporations point out that some managers are responsible for ten or more direct reports. Obviously, the larger the number of people for whom you are responsible, the greater effort it will take to keep up with their individual languages of appreciation—and to find the time to do so.

Sometimes a business is structured such that a team member actually has two or more supervisors. This happens most often when their responsibilities cross departmental boundaries. Although it is fine for more than one supervisor to encourage this worker, the situation may create a vacuum when no one takes the responsibility to encourage the worker at all.

Overcoming Structural and Procedural Issues

Structural issues can be one of the more difficult challenges to overcome because they often are embedded in the fabric of the organization. They are not just individual issues but more systemic in nature. The answer may require supervisors and higher-level managers to work together in finding a solution. The real question that needs to be answered is, "How can we best ensure that Chantel is consistently encouraged and shown appreciation? Who is the most logical person to provide this type of communication and feedback to her?"

The answer to this question takes the discussion outside of "who reports to whom." Finding the team member who has the opportunity to observe and give encouragement to Chantel, and from whom she would value receiving this type of communication, is the more important issue.

In situations where a manager supervises a large group, we have found success in helping the manager identify one or two people with whom they will start the process. Later, they can move to other team members. The employees can be selected either because they are key leaders for the unit and losing them to discouragement would be devastating to the organization, or they may be workers who are clearly currently discouraged or disconnected from their supervisor and need immediate attention. Picking one or two people to start encouraging is clearly a better option than feeling overwhelmed and not doing anything at all.

> *The real question that needs to be answered is, "How can we best ensure that Chantel is **consistently encouraged and shown appreciation?**"*

CHALLENGE #5: PERSONAL DISCOMFORT WITH COMMUNICATING APPRECIATION

We see this in two forms. The first is the age-old position of some business owners and managers: "Why should I thank them for doing their job? That is why I pay them." We find this attitude sometimes comes from senior leaders and other individuals who view themselves as self-made leaders. They were raised through difficult circumstances, often with little family support, and have become successful in their field largely due to hard work, perseverance, and personal grit. These leaders are tough minded and typically don't have a lot of focus on relationships or feelings. They view responsibility as a primary virtue and they don't look to others for thanks or appreciation. They do what they do because "we are supposed to," or "that is just what you do." Thus, they tend to hold little value for showing appreciation of any kind to others.

A variation of this position is found among driven young professionals. We have experienced resistance from bright, hardworking, Gen X and Millennial professionals. One such young woman commented to us, "I am self-motivated and I always do my best. I don't expect to be praised for doing my job, and I think this whole process is irrelevant."

> *One such young woman commented to us, "I am self-motivated and I always do my best. **I don't expect to be praised for doing my job.**"*

The second version of personal discomfort in communicating appreciation comes from individuals who have difficulty communicating on a personal level. These leaders and managers are fact oriented and task driven. They are all about "getting the work done" and are often excellent supervisors in the area of production. These individuals usually don't show much emotion aside from anger and frustration when goals are not being met. Sometimes they can be pleasant and congenial, but their focus is on "just the facts, ma'am." They find it difficult to express appreciation to colleagues. If they do so, it may come across in a very matter-of-fact manner. Often their comments are brief: "Thanks." "Good job, Amanda." "Nice work, Marcus." Then they move on to the next goal to be achieved.

These employees often don't have a wide range of emotional expression. They are appreciative but just don't think of sharing their thoughts or feelings with others. Therefore, unless prompted to do so, they rarely express appreciation to coworkers.

Overcoming Personal Discomfort

Employees who don't seem to intrinsically value showing appreciation to their colleagues may never change their viewpoint. Some people have their mind set and are not open to explore new ideas. To try to force this person to change is likely a waste of time and energy, and to do so will only result in frustration.

However, some of these individuals are "willing to listen to facts." Research indicates that communicating appreciation to employees decreases the chances of their leaving, increases customer satisfaction, and sometimes improves productivity.[3] Once they see the benefits, these leaders are willing to enthusiastically support building a climate of expressing appreciation in their organization.

For a helpful tool, see "Real Men Don't Need Encouragement (False)" in the Appreciation Toolkit at the back of this book or at appreciationatwork.com/resources.

Other leaders may be willing to "do an experiment," even if to prove you wrong. We believe that if a work group will take the **MBA Inventory** and share the results with one another, a significant number of individuals will express appreciation and thus create a more positive and productive workforce. When leaders see the results, they are likely to encourage other departments to do the same.

A second group of persons who express discomfort are those who are more introverted, less socially skilled, or not as relationally oriented. For these individuals, the task is to find the acts of encouragement and appreciation within the general parameters of their comfort zone. These team members will need more structure, more encouragement, and monitoring to make sure that they actually follow through. For them to successfully show appreciation to their colleagues, they need to start with "baby steps"—

those actions that clearly fall within their current repertoire of behavior. They need to be praised and encouraged for any action that approximates the desired behaviors. Of course, your expression of appreciation for their behavior should be expressed in the appreciation language that they prefer.

CHALLENGE #6: THE "WEIRDNESS FACTOR"

One of the interesting challenges we have encountered in working with businesses and organizations on the languages of appreciation is what we have come to call the "weirdness factor." This "weirdness" comes from the fact that everyone in the room is hearing the material on how to encourage and show appreciation to one's colleagues, and they are each working on a plan to implement the concepts in their daily work relationships—with one another! Many times at this point someone in the room says, "I'm with you on the need to do this, and I want to start using what you have taught us. But it feels kind of weird because we're all going to start encouraging one another and doing things to help out our teammates—but we all know it's part of this training. So it can feel sort of fake." And usually, most of the people in the room are nodding and agreeing.

Two issues need to be addressed here. First, there is the discomfort of starting to relate somewhat differently to one's colleagues, with everyone knowing that the impetus comes from the languages of appreciation concepts and training. This often leads to a hesitation in starting to communicate appreciation or encouragement for fear of being perceived as fake or disingenuous. "They're going to think I'm just doing this because I'm supposed to—that they're just a project to me," is a comment we sometimes hear.

The second part of the "weirdness factor" is the risk of the recipient dismissing another's act of encouragement as not being genuine, or that they are "doing it to look good in front of the boss." If people aren't careful, they can question the sincerity of their colleagues' intentions.

So there is a sense of "weirdness" created internally both within the individual who is *initiating* an act of encouragement, and within the person who may *receive* a message of appreciation. The combination of these two thought patterns, if left unaddressed, can be deadly to the process—no one does anything for fear of their actions being judged as not being authentic and genuine.

Overcoming the "Weirdness Factor"

We have found some very simple steps that can be taken that can greatly diminish the weirdness factor. First, *we acknowledge it.* As part of the process of developing action steps for each team member, if the issue hasn't come up, we bring it up. "You know, we have found that many times as we begin to talk about these ideas, people start to feel a bit weird about everyone working on encouraging one another at the same time." You can actually see and feel the level of anxiety in the room decrease significantly. (In psychological circles, this is called "normalization"—helping people realize that what they are experiencing is normal enables them to accept their situation and reactions more readily.)

Secondly, *we relate the experience to previous life experiences.* Whenever people try something new or different, the new behavior can feel a bit odd or unnatural. It doesn't "flow" initially. (There are lots of examples—learning to dribble a basketball, adjusting one's golf swing, changing one's wardrobe or hairstyle, beginning an exercise program with a trainer.) We encourage people to understand and accept the initial strangeness, but also to persevere and work through it—it usually goes away fairly quickly.

We also provide tools to get past the weirdness. It can be as simple as giving the team a sample sentence such as, "I know you may think I am doing this just because of the languages of appreciation training we have been doing, but I really do . . ." Putting the concern out front usually disarms the issue. And we also encourage the use of humor to defuse the situation. When a person is a recipient of an act of encouragement, and it is obvious to both parties that it has flowed from their training, we've encouraged team members to say something like, "Thanks, I feel *so* much better now—like I am valued and appreciated" (with a smile, not a sarcastic tone). There usually is a lot of laughter that occurs when colleagues begin to use the various languages of appreciation and the specific action steps from their teammates' list.

Finally, *we encourage everyone to give the benefit of the doubt to their coworkers and accept their actions as being genuine.* Let's be honest: It takes some courage to take a new idea and try to make it work within your daily work relationships. But having a positive attitude and thinking, "Hey, at least they are trying; I appreciate the effort," leads to positive interactions all around.

In fact, later in the training process, we repeatedly hear comments like, "I have to tell you, at first I thought this whole process was kind of weird—a bit 'touchy-feely' for me. And at the beginning, even though I knew my colleagues were saying things and doing things because it was part of this project, it still felt really good. I liked hearing the nice things they had to say." (For more on this topic, please see "Acknowledging and Dealing with the

Weirdness Factor" in the Appreciation Toolkit at the back of this book or go to appreciationatwork.com/resources.)

To Sum Up

We would be intellectually dishonest if we were to claim that *Motivating by Appreciation* is an easy process for every individual and in every setting. This is clearly not the case. There are some workers for whom encouraging colleagues will be a significant "growth-point." Some work settings have intrinsic characteristics that make communicating appreciation more difficult.

However, we have not found a company or nonprofit organization for which the *Motivating by Appreciation* concept cannot work. The challenge often requires some creative thinking and problem solving, but the problems are not insurmountable. We believe it is worth the effort to engage those with whom you work closely in an effort to enhance the level of effectiveness in expressing appreciation to each other.

MAKING IT PERSONAL

1. *On a scale of 0–10, to what degree is busyness a hindrance to your implementing the concept of Motivating by Appreciation? If busyness is a major problem for you, would you consider learning to make effective expressions of appreciation one of your priorities for the next six months?*

2. *On a scale of 0–10, how strongly do you feel that Motivating by Appreciation would enhance the work climate of your organization? If you are strongly motivated, then what will you do to encourage others to join you in this pursuit?*

3. *Do you feel that Motivating by Appreciation will not work in your organization? Why? Would you be willing to discuss the concept with at least one of your colleagues and get their opinion?*

4. *On a scale of 0–10, how overwhelmed do you feel with your existing responsibilities? If you are highly overwhelmed, perhaps this is not the best time for you to consider trying to implement the MBA concept. However, you might consider learning the primary appreciation language of at least one coworker in an attempt to be more effective in expressing appreciation to that person.*

5. *Have you discovered structural or procedural issues that inhibit effective patterns of expressing appreciation in your organization? If so, you may want to seek to implement some of the suggestions made in this chapter in overcoming those issues.*

6. On a scale of 0–10, how much personal emotional discomfort do you feel with the idea of communicating appreciation to your colleagues? If your discomfort level is high,
   can you identify why? What might you do to lower your
   level of discomfort? Remember, "baby steps" are better
   than no steps.

15

AUTHENTIC APPRECIATION:

What to Do When You Don't Appreciate Your Team Members

When we were presenting the *Motivating by Appreciation* model, one organizational leader asked, "But what if I don't really appreciate those who work for me?" Our first thought was that he was joking, but his next statement indicated that he was totally serious. "No, really; what am I supposed to do if there are people on my team that I don't appreciate? I'm not pleased with the work they're doing." We intend to answer that question in this chapter.

We have found that there are both internal and external reasons for lack of appreciation of team members. The internal reasons reside within ourselves while the external reasons are various factors in the work setting that make it difficult for us to feel appreciation toward a specific colleague. First, let us examine the internal issues.

SORTING OUT OUR OWN ISSUES

One of the most common reasons that we lack appreciation for those with whom we work is that we have unrealistic expectations of them. For a variety of reasons some individuals have extremely high expectations. Sometimes this includes high expectation for themselves. At other times, the focus is more on others. For those who have high expectations for themselves, they may experience either high self-esteem or low self-esteem. If they consistently reach their goals, they will likely feel good about themselves, be proud of themselves, and feel that they are very successful. However, if they consistently fail to live up to their expectations for themselves, they may come away with feelings of discouragement. They are saying to themselves, "I didn't do my best on that project. I don't like the way that turned out. I know I can do better than that." These people seldom feel successful because they will not allow themselves to celebrate anything less than perfection.

> *One of the most common reasons that we lack appreciation for those with whom we work is that we have **unrealistic expectations of them.***

When high expectations are focused on colleagues or the people who work under our supervision, we may well be expecting more than they can perform. Thus, no matter what a person does, it is not "good enough" for us. We are not pleased with the end product. We may criticize or make suggestions of how the task could have been done better, quicker, or more cheaply.

Some individuals who have high expectations of others are driven people who are often quite successful. These people may be business owners, managers, colleagues, customers, or vendors. Because they are driven, they naturally drive others and can sometimes be quite overbearing.

On the other hand, some people who have high expectations for others simply have a critical personality. They are not necessarily successful themselves. In fact, they may overestimate their knowledge and skills. They have developed a lifestyle of criticizing others. These people will never have good relationships for one simple reason: No one likes to be constantly criticized. (If you see yourself falling into this category, our suggestion is that as quickly as possible, you find a competent counselor who can help you understand yourself, what motivates your criticism, and how to change this destructive pattern of relating to people.)

If you find yourself dissatisfied with the performance level of a number of people who work under your supervision, it would be wise to take an honest self-assessment and see if you have unrealistically high expectations. If you quickly answer, "No, I just have high standards," you may be rushing to an inaccurate conclusion. We suggest that you ask a friend who will be honest with you this question: "Do you think that I have unrealistic expectations of others? Please give me your honest opinion." If you are really serious, you might privately ask two or three close friends the same question. Take their answers seriously because if your expectations are indeed unrealistic, you will never become an encourager because no one can please you. There is only one answer: You must minimize your expectations so that you can genuinely appreciate the hard work of those you supervise.

Another reason people do not appreciate the work of others is *personal irritations*. We react negatively to someone, not because they aren't doing their job, but because there is something about them that rubs us the wrong way. The irritation might stem from some aspect of their personality. In your opinion they may "talk too much" or "they can't carry on a conversation." It may be that their work space always looks disorganized or you may resent the fact that they consistently show up for work ten minutes late and leave ten minutes early. Perhaps you are annoyed that they seem to always be happy. You can't believe that anyone could be that happy all the time. Conversely, you may say to yourself, "Every day they look like their best friend just died."

The irritation may also come from the way they do things. The way they approach a task is exactly the opposite of the way you approach the same task. You may resent the fact that they like to listen to music while they work. The earbud in their ear makes you think they are not giving their full attention to their work. Every time you see it, you get irritated. Or perhaps you get irritated because of the way they dress. In your opinion, their dress is inappropriate for their job.

> The reality is **people are different.** In the work setting, the question is, **"Are they performing their job** in a satisfactory manner?"

Sometimes it's simply that the person's lifestyle is different from your own. You can't imagine why they would wear rings in their nose or have tattoos on their arms or a hairstyle that, to you, is barbaric. Sometimes it is generational differences that irritate us. The middle-aged single mother is disturbed by the young "macho" single male who acts like the world revolves around him.

There are many things that may spark personal irritations. This is true in all human relationships. The reality is people are different. In the work setting, the question is, "Are they performing their job in a satisfactory manner?" If the answer is yes, then you can genuinely express appreciation to them for their work even though you may be irritated by other issues. If the answer is no, and you are the supervisor, then you need to address the problem of work performance.

The truth is we cannot change individuals' personalities and lifestyle patterns so that everyone looks and acts like us. We have to accept human differences and look for ways to encourage those whose behavior may genuinely irritate us but whose work performance is positive.

Another reason some supervisors have difficulty expressing appreciation is that they have *inadequate information*. We have found some supervisors do not appreciate team members whom they do not directly supervise because they don't fully understand the individual's responsibilities. There is a lack of information resulting from poor communication patterns within the organization. One supervisor, Rob, said, "I don't get what Chris does. All I see him doing is flitting here and there, going from one office to another. I thought he was our IT guy. Shouldn't he be in his office making sure the computer system works correctly?"

Sasha, the director of information systems, responded to Rob, "Chris is our network specialist and his first responsibility is to make sure that each person's computer is hooked up to the computer network properly so they can communicate with everyone else. The reason you see him going place to place is because he is responding to calls for help from people whose computers aren't working correctly. He goes to see them personally, hears what their problem is, and fixes it. He is doing exactly what he is supposed to do. And he is doing it well."

"Ohhh. Okay, if that is what he is supposed to be doing—

great!" Rob replied, somewhat sheepishly.

If you have a question about the work performance of someone who does not work under your direct supervision, it is always wise to talk to the person to whom the employee reports. You may find that your concern is simply due to lack of information. When Rob encountered Chris in the hallway two days later, he said, "Chris, I hear good things about your work from Sasha. I appreciate what you are doing for the company." Chris walked away feeling affirmed. Rob was able to express genuine appreciation because he took time to get information.

There may be other internal issues that keep individuals from giving authentic appreciation, but these are the three most common that we have encountered. Now let's turn to external issues.

IF THE ISSUE IS PERFORMANCE

Often, we find that a manager is not pleased with a person on her staff for good reason. It is not related to some internal thought pattern on the part of the manager. There is an objective factor behind the manager's lack of appreciation for the colleague. The employee may not be performing the job adequately. This happens in almost every organization. Some individuals simply are not doing their jobs at an acceptable level of quality.

There may be many reasons for this lack of performance. Here are three of the most common factors we have discovered. First, the employee may have *personal problems at home*. It is well known that when people are going through a divorce, their performance on the job is adversely affected. When adults have children who are in trouble with the law or are abusing drugs, it often negatively affects the employee's work performance. A single adult who has recently experienced the breakup of a long-term dating relationship may be distracted from work responsibilities.

On the other hand, the employee may have *physical problems*. Employees who live with chronic pain or are on medication for various conditions can face challenges in the workplace that may not be readily apparent to others.

Or, some employees may simply have a *low work ethic*. They have developed an attitude that says, "Only do what is necessary." They may simply be enduring the job in order to keep food on the table.

> *Many managers* **do not like confrontation** *and will go for months* **avoiding the issue** *of a low-performing employee.*

A manager has no way of knowing what is motivating poor performance unless the manager asks the employee. Many managers do not like confrontation and will go for months avoiding the issue of a low-performing employee. Unfortunately, this does not resolve the situation, and the manager becomes increasingly frustrated. Such a manager will have a hard time expressing appreciation to this employee.

Our suggestion is that the manager should have an open, honest conversation with the individual. The approach needs to be kind but straightforward. You might say something like this: "Jen, I have observed in recent weeks that you have not been performing to your potential on the job. This concerns me. I know there is probably an explanation, and that is why I wanted to talk with you. Is there something going on in your life that is contributing to your decreased performance? If so, I want to do anything I can to help you." Such a caring approach will likely bring the manager an honest answer.

With this information, the manager can then be helpful to the employee. One manager who had such a conversation with an administrative assistant discovered that the employee's son was on drugs. She was able to help the employee find an affordable treatment program for her son and in the process deepen their friendship and increase the employee's productivity. Then the manager was able to express authentic appreciation. The administrative assistant then reciprocated genuine appreciation to the manager.

Another reason people do not perform satisfactorily is that *they have not been adequately trained for their responsibilities.* In our experience, we have found this is a common reason for low performance on the job. The supervisor either assumed the employee had the skill and knowledge base, or believed they would pick it up on their own. In a few weeks or months, colleagues notice that the employee is not completing the task on a satisfactory level. This reality often goes unobserved by the supervisor because he assumes that the human resources department has adequately screened new employees. However, few employees arrive on the scene with all the skills and information needed to adequately perform their jobs.

When a supervisor or manager realizes that the person does not have the information or training necessary to perform the job, the most positive response is to provide the training. Such training may come in many venues. It may mean allowing the employee to work with a more skilled employee for a few days for on-the-job training. Or, it may mean requiring the employee to take classes at the local technical institute where, on their own time and at their own expense, they learn the skills required for the job. If an employee is unwilling to accept the training that is offered, then in our opinion the supervisor has no option but to begin the process of releasing the employee.

In today's world, most employees are willing to take training opportunities in order to keep their job. Once a manager sees the person taking the initiative to learn and consequently raising their performance level, the manager can then honestly give authentic appreciation to the employee. In this case, the employee feels encouraged and motivated to continue reaching their potential on the job.

A third common reason for low job performance is that the organization *does not have in place an effective process for review, feedback, instruction, and correction.* In our work with businesses, one of the most common deficits we observed is the lack of established processes for reviewing employees' performance, giving them regular feedback, and providing corrective instruction. This is a formula for frustration, both for the team member and supervisor.

All of us have "growth areas." Supervisors and team members need regular times to communicate with each other about what is going well and what can be improved. When there is not a structured process in place, this type of communication often does not occur.

Thus, the supervisor is dissatisfied with the team member's performance and likely will have great difficulty expressing to them genuine appreciation. They are, in fact, frustrated with the employee. Since there is no set time for regular feedback, the weeks come and go while the supervisor's frustration intensifies. The employee may or may not know of the supervisor's dissatisfaction but they are certainly not receiving encouraging words from the supervisor.

If your company does not have such an evaluation communication process in place, we suggest that you talk with the person in the company who directly supervises your own work. Share the concept and let them share it with their supervisors. If the concern arises from employees, wise business managers will listen and likely initiate such a process.

*To ask, "**What am I doing well** and what can I improve?" is a **positive step.***

In the meantime, an employee may request feedback from their immediate supervisor. To ask, "What am I doing well and what can I improve?" is a positive step. This is an informal way for the employee to get feedback and correction before an issue mushrooms into a major problem. Most supervisors are willing to give this kind of feedback if the employee requests it. When they see your efforts to make positive changes, they are likely to begin to give you genuine expressions of appreciation.

On the other hand, a manager who is unhappy with the performance of an employee can also informally initiate the process by simply saying to the individual: "I would like to get your suggestions on what I could do to make you more successful in your position." Listen carefully to the employee's suggestion. It may give you a clue as to the reason for their low performance. If their suggestion seems reasonable, implement it. In the context of caring conversation, you can then give the employee honest feedback about your observations and suggestions on what they might do to enhance work performance.

What we are saying is that if a company does not have a process of review, feedback, and corrective instruction, it can be done in an informal manner. Once the employee responds positively, the manager is now able to give genuine expressions of appreciation.

To Sum Up

We have found that encouraging teams of employees and supervisors to take the **Motivating by Appreciation Inventory** often highlights other issues that need to be addressed. In fact, we openly encourage supervisors not to attempt communicating appreciation if they truly do not appreciate the team member. Most people have very sensitive receptors to insincere forms of communication. Going through the motions of communicating appreciation when there is not a genuine basis for it will do real harm to the relationship between the supervisor and the team member.

It is far better to wait—and deal with the root issues. If the supervisor realizes that the problem is an issue within herself, then she must identify what is keeping her from giving genuine appreciation. (Please see "Can Praise Be a Problem?" in the Appreciation Toolkit at the back of this book or go to appreciationatwork.com/resources.)

> *We openly encourage supervisors not to attempt communicating appreciation if they truly do not **appreciate the team member.***

On the other hand, if the supervisor concludes that the issue is one of the three external factors that we have discussed, he must directly address the personal issues of the team member, provide more training for the employee, or seek to establish a regular process of giving corrective feedback to the individual.

One final note: In today's corporate world, executive coaching has become a popular approach to help supervisors analyze and solve relational problems. A qualified coach can assist the manager in evaluating how realistic their expectations are, or help them deal with personal issues the manager may have with the employee. Most supervisors can strengthen their own people skills by enlisting the help of such a coach.

MAKING IT PERSONAL

1. *Are there individuals who work under your supervision for whom you find it difficult, if not impossible, to express authentic appreciation?*

2. *If you are not a manager, do you have coworkers you honestly do not appreciate?*

Internal Issues

3. *Would you be willing to do the following exercise? Put the name of the person you do not appreciate at the top of a sheet of paper. (You may have additional sheets for additional coworkers.) Reflect on the possibility that your lack of appreciation grows from internal issues by answering the following questions.*

   a. *Could it be possible that you have unrealistic expectations of the employee?*

   b. *Is your lack of appreciation growing out of personal irritations with the individual? If your answer is yes, what are the specific things that irritate you?*

   • *Is it likely that the person can or will change these points of irritation?*

- *Do you think you could come to accept these factors as simply being a part of who they are and affirm them for their work even though you find certain things about them irritating?*

  c. *Could it be possible that your irritation is growing out of the fact that you do not have information about what the employee is supposed to be doing in their job? If your answer is yes, how could you find that information?*

External Issues

4. *Have you concluded that the reason you cannot express appreciation is that the person simply is not performing their job adequately? If your answer is yes, would you be willing to engage that employee in a conversation in an effort to find out what is going on in their lives that keeps them from reaching their potential?*

5. *Could it be possible that the person has not been adequately trained for their responsibilities? If so, what steps might you take to help them get the training they need?*

6. *If your organization does not have in place an effective process for review, feedback, and corrective instruction, what steps might you take informally or formally to make this a reality in your organization?*

7. *If you are a supervisor, have you considered the possibility of some sessions with an executive coach to enhance your own leadership skills?*

Now It's Your Turn

Communicating appreciation and encouragement to one's fellow workers is a powerful tool in influencing your organization positively—regardless of your position within the system. We are well aware, however, that the ability and willingness to show appreciation and communicate encouragement is not a magic bullet that will solve all of the challenges within a workplace.

We acknowledge that a healthy work environment will be characterized by a number of factors, including:

- Quality team members
- Effective communication skills and procedures set in place to facilitate regular communication
- Trusting relationships
- Common vision and goals among team members

- Standardized processes and procedures, including standards to be met and ongoing monitoring of performance
- Healthy methods for correction and conflict resolution
- Clear lines of responsibility, including accountability and rewards for results

The more these characteristics exist in an organization, the more likely the organization will meet its goals and the team members will enjoy their work.

We also know that no organization is perfect. Each has it own unique strengths and weaknesses. But we have found that when the members of an organization engage in communicating appreciation and encouragement in the ways that are most meaningful to their team members, then good things happen:

- Interactions between colleagues take on a more positive tone.
- Relational tensions that have existed begin to decrease.
- Employees (and volunteers) report that the workplace environment becomes more enjoyable.
- Quality team members (including volunteers) stay with the organization longer.
- The work produced is of higher quality.
- Customers begin to report higher levels of satisfaction in their interactions with the organization.

APPRECIATION, VITAMINS, AND ANTIBIOTICS

Let us share with you a word picture that we have found helpful to illustrate the power of encouragement and appreciation in transforming work-based relationships. The consistent use of encouragement (coming alongside a team member and encouraging them to persevere) and appreciation (communicating a sense of value for the work they have done and the character qualities they demonstrate) are a lot like vitamins and antibiotics.

Both are chemicals that help our physical bodies maintain health. Taking vitamins regularly is a proactive habit that provides the building blocks for developing healthy bodies. When a wound has occurred, antibiotics are chemical compounds that fight off an infection. Both have their place in keeping our bodies healthy.

Some interesting characteristics should be noted about vitamins and antibiotics. First, the chemicals that make up vitamins and/or antibiotics are typically not so powerful that one dosage meets the need the body has (there are some very strong antibiotics, but these are the exception rather than the rule). Taking a vitamin (or even a host of them) once really will not affect your physical system much. Their power and influence are a result of a series of small actions occurring consistently over time. Faithfully taking a daily multiple vitamin over a long period of time can help provide the chemicals that you need to develop a healthy body. Similarly, when an infection is developing, the repeated use of an antibiotic is needed to heal the wound or condition.

Second, different people need a variety of elements in varying amounts to maintain health. There is not a "one size fits all" multivitamin supplement that meets everyone's needs. Some people need more calcium; some need more iron; others need fairly obscure trace minerals. And there is not just one antibiotic that is suited to kill all the bacteria that can create infections. A topical antibiotic can help a skin cut heal, while another type of antibiotic is needed to fight strep throat. And it is critical to use the right chemical in the right situation. If we don't, the body doesn't get the nutrients or support it needs to be healthy.

Finally, vitamins and antibiotics are undramatic. It can be easy to forget to take your vitamin or apply the antibiotic to a wound. And missing a day or two probably won't hurt you significantly. But if you consistently and repeatedly forget to take the vitamins you need, or stop taking your antibiotic as prescribed, over time the health of your body will almost certainly be affected negatively.

So it is with appreciation and encouragement. A single act of encouragement doesn't look like it is going to change the world or make a real difference in a colleague's life. But when appreciation and encouragement are consistently communicated over a long period of time, in ways that are important to the individual—the impact can be dramatic. And when an organization is composed of healthy parts communicating effectively, and when a physical system is equipped with defenses to fight off unhealthy invaders, it can mean the difference between surviving difficult times and succumbing to a general lack of health.

"TAKING IT TO THE STREETS": APPLYING THE CONCEPTS IN YOUR WORKPLACE

It is our desire that, regardless of your position within your organization, you will take the information provided in this book and apply it to your daily relationships. We have seen individual employees make a real difference in their workplace by beginning to encourage and show appreciation to their colleagues. If you find it helpful, you may want to share your **MBA Inventory** report with your supervisor and encourage them to explore further. You might share the Appreciation Toolkit at the back of the book with them. Our experience has been that often the supervisor becomes intrigued, contacts us, and begins to take their team through the five languages of appreciation process. Sometimes this has begun on a departmental level. In a number of organizations and businesses, the process has grown and spread organically throughout the entire organization.

KATHY: "I THOUGHT I KNEW MY TEAM MEMBERS"

Let us share one final example. As a district supervisor for an international social service agency, Kathy was aware of the need to develop a leadership training process for her key leaders across a three-state region. Given that the organization was nonprofit, the team members were there largely out of a sense of calling to serve others. Although her team was generally healthy, she knew that they were at risk for burning out due to the ongoing demands of the work they did and the limited resources of the organization. Through a leadership training course Kathy was taking, she became aware of the *5 Languages of Appreciation in the Workplace* project. She felt that her leaders needed encouragement and support, but she sensed that she was not hitting the mark in her efforts.

We arranged to do an introductory session via videoconference for her team members who were spread across a number of offices. We introduced the motivating by appreciation concepts to the team and had each of the team members (approximately ten) take the **MBA Inventory**. We conducted a follow-up videoconference to go over their results to more fully explain the languages of appreciation in daily life, and helped them develop initial action plans for implementing the process. We shared with her team members a group chart showing each individual's primary language, secondary language, and least important language. We continued to follow up with email reminders and suggestions for them to try, every two weeks for three months.

The results were significant. Kathy shared with us that knowing how to specifically encourage her team members greatly enhanced her efforts at expressing appreciation. She also developed a list of the preferred action items for each of the team members' primary languages of appreciation. This gave her team specific information on how best to express appreciation to team members.

Later Kathy said, "I thought I knew my team members and what was important to them, since we had worked together a number of years. However, I realized that I was off-base with a number of them. Having them identify their preferred languages of appreciation and especially including the specific action items important to them has made it far easier for me to hit the mark, even across long distances."

She continued, "The changes in our team are remarkable. We get along better and genuinely appreciate each other more. I am seeing the team members reach out and encourage others when they see someone struggling. It has become a 'fun thing' for us—learning how to effectively communicate appreciation."

While we were working with Kathy, she was promoted to a new supervisory position of a larger district. Kathy told us, "I am going to use the *MBA* with my new team. There is a huge need. The relationships aren't as healthy—a lot of internal competition with some bickering. They need help and tools in how to communicate more positively with one another. I can't wait to see what's going to happen. Let's get going!" We are currently working with Kathy in accomplishing this goal.

GET GOING!

One of the chief lessons that we have learned in working with diverse types of organizations and a broad spectrum of team members is the following principle:

The primary difference between a successful plan and a plan that fails is the degree to which the plan is actually tried, corrective actions are taken as needed, and the plan continues to be implemented over time.

Communicating appreciation and encouragement effectively isn't rocket science. The ideas are not that hard to understand intellectually. The keys to success, like in most behavioral change, are to actually *start* to apply the concepts, "get back on the horse" when you fail to keep working the plan, and be committed to persevering over the long haul. Then you will see the positive benefits of your efforts.

We believe that the desire to work (engaging in meaningful, productive activity—whether paid or not paid) is innately in the nature of being human. And the experience of enjoying one's work comes from a combination of factors: our own attitudes, practicing healthy habits within relationships, being affirmed and valued by others, and acknowledging that enjoying one's work is a gift given by our Creator.

It is our desire that thousands of employees and volunteers will find the concepts of this book to be a significant tool to help them create a more positive workplace. We believe that enhancing the emotional climate in an organization will help the organization more effectively reach its goals. If people enjoy their work and feel appreciated by supervisors and colleagues, they are far more likely to have organizational loyalty and work hard to help the organization continue to be successful.

If you have found this book helpful, we hope that you will share it with your friends in other organizations—and also share your thoughts and success stories on our website (appreciationatwork. com). By effectively communicating appreciation and encouragement to others, you can be the impetus that creates a more positive work environment for yourself and those around you.

Notes

Introduction

1. Mike Robbins, *Focus on the Good Stuff: The Power of Appreciation* (San Francisco: Jossey-Bass, 2000), 32.

Chapter 1: *Motivating by Appreciation: The Concept*

1. Jan Watson and Christine Lapointe, "Motivation through Recognition & Reward," *Review of Ophthalmology* 12 (May 16, 2005): 29–30.
2. Steven R. Covey, *The 7 Habits of Highly Effective People* (New York: Free Press, 1989), 241.
3. Marcus Buckingham and Donald O. Clifton, *Now, Discover Your Strengths* (New York: Free Press, 2001), 171.

Chapter 2: *For Business Leaders: Understanding the Return on Investment from Appreciation and Encouragement*

1. Leigh Branham, *The 7 Hidden Reasons Employees Leave: How to Recognize the Subtle Signs and Act before It's Too Late* (New York: AMACOM, 2005), 24.
2. Gallup Q4 in FSA, US Department of Agriculture Farm and Foreign Agricultural Services; http://hr.ffas.usda.gov/Internet/FSA_File/q4.doc.
3. Subhasn C. Kundu and Jay A. Vora, "Creating a Talented Workforce for Delivering Service Quality," *Human Resource Planning* 27, no. 2 (2004): 40–51.

4. John R. Darling and Michael J. Keeffe, "Entrepreneurial Leadership Strategies and Values: Keys to Operational Excellence," *Journal of Small Business and Entrepreneurship* 20 (2007): 41–54.

5. Fred Luthans, Kyle W. Luthans, Richard M. Hodgetts, and Brett C. Luthans, "Positive Approach to Leadership (PAL) Implications for Today's Organizations," *Journal of Leadership Studies* 8 (2001): 3–20.

6. Paul E. Spector, *Job Satisfaction: Application, Assessment, Causes, and Consequences* (Thousand Oaks, CA: Sage Publications, 1997); Gary P. Latham, ed., *Work Motivation: History, Theory, Research, and Practice* (Thousand Oaks, CA: Sage Publications, 2007).

7. Sami M. Abbasi and Kenneth W. Hollman, "Turnover: The Real Bottom Line," *Public Personnel Management* (2000): 29.

8. J. Fitz-Eng, "It's Costly to Lose Good Employees," *Workforce* (August 1997): 50.

9. T. Oh, "Employee Retention: Managing Your Turnover Drivers," *HR Focus* 73, no. 3 (March 1996): 12.

10. Gary E. Weiss and Sean A. Lincoln, "Departing Employee Can Be Nightmare," *Electronic News* (1991, reprinted March 16, 1998): 1.

11. Rudy Karsan, "Calculating the Cost of Turnover," *Employment Relations Today* 34 (2007): 33–36.

12. Brian S. Young, Stephen Worchel, and David J. Woehr, "Organizational Commitment among Public Service Employees," *Public Personnel Management* 27, no. 3 (1998): 339–48.

13. Jeffrey Pfeffer, *The Human Equation: Building Profits by Putting People First* (Boston: Harvard Business School, 1998).

14. Go to www.appreciationatwork.com/resources for more information on resources and consultants available.

Chapter 7: *Appreciation Language #5: Physical Touch*

1. Robert T. Golembiewski, *Handbook of Organizational Consultation*, 2nd ed. (New York: Marcel Dekker, 2000).

2. Jonathan Levav and Jennifer J. Argo, "Physical Contact and Financial Risk Taking," *Psychological Science* vol. 21, no. 6 (June 2010).

Chapter 11: *Motivating by Appreciation in Various Industry Sectors*

1. Robert Roy Johnson, "Supervising with Emotion," *Law & Order* 55, no. 2 (2007): 12–14.

2. Nona Momeni, "The Relation between Managers' Emotional Intelligence and the Organizational Climate They Create," *Public Personnel Management* 38 (2009).

3. Michael D. Akers and Grover L. Porter, "Your EQ skills: Got what it takes? So you thought the CPA exam was your last test? Read on," *Journal of Accountancy* 195 (2003): 65–66.

4. Visit www.mbainventory.com and click on the "International versions" button to see what translations are currently available.

Chapter 12: *The Unique Characteristics of Volunteer Settings*

1. John Wilson, "Volunteering," *Annual Review of Sociology* 26 (2000): 215–40.

Chapter 14: *Motivating by Appreciation: Overcoming Your Challenges*

1. Steven R. Covey, A. Roger Merrill, and Rebecca R. Merrill, *First Things First* (New York: Fireside, 1994).

2. Steven R. Covey, *The 7 Habits of Highly Effective People* (New York: Fireside, 1989).

3. Richard S. Allen and Marilyn M. Helms, "Employee Perceptions of the Relationship between Strategy, Rewards and Organizational Performance," *Journal of Business Strategies* 1 (2002)

APPRECIATION TOOLKIT:

Resources to Use and Share with Others

As we have worked with businesses and organizations on the *Motivating by Appreciation* model, we have found that certain issues and questions come up repeatedly. So we have developed a series of stand-alone pieces that address these frequently asked questions. In addition to being available here in the book, we have made each of these pieces available online (www.appreciationatwork.com), so you may easily print them out in hard copy form and share them with others. We also have created video clips that address many of the topics, and these are available on the website as well.

Here we explore such questions as:

- How do I know when my team needs to feel appreciated?
- What's the best (and most cost-effective) way to give gifts?
- Do men really need encouragement?
- What about volunteers?
- We hope these will be helpful to you and your team.

Picking Up Some Not-so-subtle Cues That Your Colleagues Need to Feel Appreciated

You may be surrounded by coworkers who need to be encouraged—and you may not know it. Not everyone wears a sign that says, "I need to feel valued" or "Approaching burnout: encouragement needed."

Some of us, of course, do wear "signs" on our faces where others can easily tell when we are discouraged or weary. (And, hopefully, our colleagues respond to our indirect requests for help.) But many people are harder to read. And some of us are not especially talented at picking up cues sent out by others. They may be clearly communicating their distress, but we are missing the signals.

Here are some cues that you can watch for, to help you know when those with whom you work may need a message of appreciation or encouragement:

DISCOURAGEMENT

Discouragement literally means "lack of courage." Sometimes people "lose heart" over time. They begin to wonder why they should keep trying. When you hear people make statements like "Why try? It won't matter," or "I'm ready to give up and just call it quits," you should know that a sense of discouragement is setting in.

IRRITABILITY AND RESISTANCE

When team members are chronically irritable, it usually means they are upset or angry about something. It may be work related—or it may be due to personal issues. But the problem is more intense when the employee shows resistance—for example, resistance to instruction and new procedures, or resistance to change.

Often workers become irritable and resistant when they don't feel valued by others for what they do.

INCREASED ABSENTEEISM OR TARDINESS

Some people send indirect messages when they are unhappy. Not showing up regularly for work or consistently arriving late is one way to indirectly say, "I don't want to be here," or, "I don't feel like I really matter around here." While the pattern of lateness or absenteeism needs to be addressed directly by the individual's supervisor, management also needs to reaffirm the employee's significance to the organization—that he or she does, indeed, matter.

CYNICISM AND SARCASM

We frequently hear managers report concerns about how cynical their staff has become. Sarcastic responses to new processes and procedures can become commonplace. Cynicism and sarcasm often betray underlying anger and mistrust. But a steady diet of authentic appreciation can begin to turn around office negativism.

APATHY AND PASSIVITY

People become passive when they believe their actions don't matter, and that whatever they may try won't make a difference. Apathy (a "why should I try?" attitude) often breeds passivity. Workers begin to put forth less effort when they believe their supervisor or colleagues don't value what they do. When you observe increased passivity among your team members, take note, because poorer work performance is not far behind.

SOCIAL WITHDRAWAL

A clear warning sign of a colleague not feeling like they are valued and part of the team is when they begin to withdraw socially. Coworkers who become less communicative, don't "hang out" as much, decline invitations to go out for lunch or after work, and also just aren't as involved as they used to be, are often separating themselves from the rest of the team. They often withdraw because they feel no one cares about them. These individuals need to be encouraged and feel valued by others.

NEGATIVE WORK ENVIRONMENT

Finally, when the overall work environment is characterized by negative communication styles, then encouragement and appreciation are in dire need by all. Positive comments between colleagues can, over time, decrease cutting remarks, intense negative reactions, and overly critical feedback among team members—but a sustained, concerted effort is needed.

SUMMARY

If you pay attention, your colleagues often are sending clear signals that they need to feel valued by those with whom they work. Utilizing the various languages of appreciation, and specific action steps they have identified as being meaningful to them, will provide the best results for "hitting the target."

Doing so will help the morale within the workplace environment, and will also provide the foundation for your coworkers to feel like they are a valued part of the team. The results will become evident and beneficial to all.

www.appreciationatwork.com

How to Reward Volunteers

Volunteers can be both the easiest and hardest team members to encourage and show appreciation to. They are easy to encourage because often their expectations aren't very high (with the exception of adolescent volunteers!), and, therefore, any positive communication is received well.

But volunteers are also difficult to show appreciation to, for a variety of reasons. First, they often aren't around very often. They may come to help weekly, monthly, or just for special events. And when they are present, there is usually plenty of work to do and the supervisor is busy managing lots of people. Second, unless they have been volunteering for a long time (which is the exception rather than the rule), the persons who are supervising don't typically get to know the individual volunteers very well. So you don't know how best to encourage them.

We have found it helpful for organizations, as part of their orientation for volunteers, to give the **MBA Inventory** and then introduce the appreciation languages concept. We have successfully used this as part of the kickoff process at the beginning of the organization's service year* (for example, in the fall at the beginning of the school year). It immediately communicates to your volunteers that you value them and want to know how to encourage them in their service.

But if you need some short fill-in-the-gap suggestions of how to encourage and show support to your volunteers, here are some suggestions you can implement right away:

- Give positive verbal encouragement to them frequently.
- Tell them "Thanks" often and immediately.
- Reinforce positive behaviors you want others to emulate.

- Use people as positive examples—tell stories about them.

- Praise them in front of team members or the people they are serving.

- Learn their name and use it.

- Go to talk with them as they arrive, and show up at the end of the day before they leave.

- Look them in the eye when talking to them.

- Give them clear instructions and standards for what is expected for a "job well done" and then give them encouragement as they try to meet the standard.

- Ask or assess what they are good at, and what they like to do. If possible, match their abilities and interests with similar tasks.

- Work alongside them. As you do, get to know them better.

- Ask if there is anything they need that would help their work go better.

- Give them a small gift that has the organization's logo or tagline on it (but make sure it is something they need or value), giving them more of a sense of connection with the organization.

- Have volunteers work together in small teams rather than individually.

- Provide snacks and refreshments during or after their time of service.

- Spend some individual time with them. Give them an opportunity to ask you questions about the organization and your role in it.

- Give them a vision of how what they are doing ties into the broader goals of the organization and helps you toward what you are trying to accomplish.

If your organization works with a significant number of volunteers, having your staff go through the Appreciation at Work *five-week training series can be an excellent way to increase your retention rate of volunteers. Go to www.appreciationatwork.com/resources for more information.*

www.appreciationatwork.com

The Art of Giving a Gift without Buying a "Thing"

G ift giving, especially in work-based relationships, is largely becoming a thing of the past. Whether for a special work anni-
versary (for example, having worked at the company for five years),
one's birthday, or to show appreciation for one's work, businesses
and organizations used to give gifts to show honor to their staff. But
this practice is less common than it used to be.

There are several reasons for this change:

- The number of meaningless token gifts we have received in the
  past has given "gifts" a negative connotation.

- We often don't know what our colleagues would want.

- Most people don't need more "things" (who needs another
  coffee mug?).

- The gifts that would be meaningful to them are often expensive
  and not within our (or the organization's) budget.

- Because of some abuses in the marketplace, there is fear of
  being accused of using gifts as a form of bribery or undue
  influence.

- Most of us don't have the time or energy to do a lot of shopping.

Yet the fact remains that a good number of the people we work
with still value receiving gifts as an expression of appreciation—it
may even be their preferred language of appreciation. So how do we
meet that need? Here are a few ideas:

1. If you haven't already, identify those team members who have *Tangible Gifts* as their primary or secondary language of appreciation. (Note: Few people tend to have *Tangible Gifts* as their primary language, so it is important to look at secondary languages on your team's chart.) Often people value gifts (as long as it isn't their lowest language), they just tend to value the other languages more.

2. Over time, take note of those activities that your coworkers like to do in their spare time. This will give you a good indication of their interests. See if they enjoy watching sports (and which teams), or if they prefer the arts, outdoor activities, or perhaps reading. Also listen (and even inquire) about where they like to go out for dinner or dessert.

3. As we noted in the chapter on the language of tangible gifts, people in our culture tend to value experiences more than things. Often these experiences have at least a small financial cost associated with them. So an easy way to give a colleague a gift is to provide the funds to do (or get) something they would enjoy. Most of us aren't comfortable with giving (or receiving) cash, so the best way to do this is through giving gift cards, tickets, or gift certificates. Anything from Amazon to iTunes to a day spa to a college sporting event would be appreciated, depending on the recipient's interest.

Happy shopping!

www.appreciationatwork.com

Can Praise Be a Problem?

Communicating appreciation and encouragement to your colleagues can actually backfire and create more problems, as in these situations:

When a relationship is tense. If you are in a work relationship that has been tense in the past, trying to communicate appreciation without acknowledging the previous issues will most probably lead to a cool reception of the message.

When you move too fast. Sometimes, in the normal course of a workday, we have difficult conversations with our colleagues. We may disagree with a decision or have to confront someone on their lack of follow-through. While it is appropriate to have these conversations, moving too quickly to try to express your appreciation for your colleague will feel awkward and disjointed.

When you change too quickly. Some individuals, in an attempt to respond positively to instruction, can try to change their behavior too abruptly. For instance, a formerly reserved, distant supervisor might be encouraged to be more outgoing, and suddenly become effusive with praise—to the point you don't recognize this new person.

When you say different things in different settings. If you chew out one of your team members in a private conversation and then later praise them in front of others, you can appear two-faced and as if you're trying to impress others, especially if the message is given in front of higher-ups.

When your words say one thing and your expression another. It's a little like the child who is forced by their parents to say, "I'm sorry," when their tone of voice, lack of eye contact, and angry expression don't convince you they mean it. Expressing appreciation when you don't look appreciative will come across as insincere.

When the object of your appreciation has been "burned" by others. Unfortunately, a number of people in the workforce have had difficult lives—growing up in dysfunctional families, experiencing abusive relationships, or being mistreated by previous employers. People in these situations are often self-protective and distrustful. They see any positive actions by others as an attempt to take advantage of them.

When the message of appreciation follows staff layoffs or pay reductions. When an organization or company has to downsize because of financial difficulties, or if staff salaries have had to be reduced, efforts at encouragement or being upbeat will fall flat. Employees are hurting, anxious, and fearful for the future, and may be grieving the loss of close colleagues. If a supervisor tries to be overly positive in the midst of difficult times, he can be perceived either as insensitive and crass, or as disingenuous and fake.

HOW DO YOU AVOID THESE PITFALLS?

1. **Check your motives.** Try to only communicate authentic, genuine appreciation.

2. **Be aware of the context.** While expressing appreciation or encouragement is usually beneficial, there are times and settings where it is better to wait.

3. **"Check in" with a trusted colleague.** If in doubt—either of the timing, your message, or how it may be received—first, touch base with someone who knows you and the situation well and

who will give you honest feedback. They may be able to give you some tips on how or when would be best to share your message.

4. **If in doubt, wait.** Almost always, taking time to assess a situation and making sure that the message will be received well is worth the wait. A delayed message communicated well and received well is far better than a rushed message that misfires.

www.appreciationatwork.com

Why Your Least Valued Appreciation Language Can Affect Your Career the Most

A good manager pays attention to the needs of their team members. Generally speaking, we are most in tune with those who are similar to us—so it's obviously easier for us to communicate appreciation and encouragement to others with primary and secondary languages of appreciation similar to ours.

But as a result, we are less likely to communicate effectively in the language that is *least* important to us personally, and this can have challenging consequences for the manager.

This language doesn't flow naturally for us. We are more likely to miss the subtle cues sent by our colleagues who value this language. So we are at risk for not encouraging and showing appreciation to these team members in ways that are important to them. We are more likely to communicate in our preferred languages, but those are not as meaningful to these colleagues.

Over time these colleagues will feel undervalued and unappreciated. We will become frustrated because we are trying to show appreciation but it is missing the mark. Eventually these employees' work performance will suffer, negative communication around the team will increase, and we may even lose valuable team members.

Fortunately, there are actions to take that can counter this process.

1. Acknowledge that your least valued language of appreciation isn't that important to you, *and* that it is a potential Achilles' heel in your relationships with others.

2. Identify those colleagues for whom your least valued language is their primary or secondary language.

3. Make a list of the specific actions that are important to each team member (for example, *affirming words*). Have it easily accessible to you throughout the day.

4. Create an action list with related time frame for you to take specific actions with these team members (e.g., schedule a weekly reminder to show up on your calendar). If you don't, you will forget to do something in their language!

5. Check in with them occasionally to see if they are feeling supported by you, and if there are better ways you can show your appreciation for them. (Remember, this is a needed area of growth for you.)

SUMMARY

Needless to say, those supervisors and managers who have team members who are not working up to their potential, who create a negative work environment, and who leave the organization dissatisfied typically will not be as successful in their organization as those who have well-functioning and highly productive teams with long-term team members. *It is important to you and your career* to pay attention to your least valued language of appreciation and how it impacts your relationships with your colleagues. By taking a few proactive steps, you can actually use this blind spot to your benefit to grow into a more effective manager.

www.appreciationatwork.com

Acknowledging and Dealing with the "Weirdness Factor"

Q. What is the "weirdness factor"?

A. The "weirdness factor" is a common reaction among work teams when the appreciation languages are first introduced and teams begin to implement the concepts.

Q. What are the most common signs of people feeling "weird" about the appreciation process?

A. Fear. Fear is the most common symptom associated with the weirdness factor. Fear that others will think you are communicating appreciation "just because we are supposed to." Fear that people will think your communication is not authentic or genuine. Fear that your encouragement won't go well or be received positively. The second most common aspect of the weirdness factor is awkwardness. We are asking individuals to try something new, and people almost always feel unnatural when trying a new behavior.

Q. Why does it occur?

A. Most people want to be viewed positively by others. We don't like others to question our motives, so we will tend to wait to do something until we feel like others believe we are doing it for the right reason. Secondly, we don't want to embarrass ourselves by doing something we feel uncomfortable doing. So we wait until it "feels more natural"—which rarely occurs without practice.

Q. What can be done to reduce the "weirdness" people may experience?

A. Acknowledge it. "Okay, we're all feeling a bit weird about this." Then, dive in anyway—waiting doesn't make the weirdness go away. Often, we encourage people to use lead-in phrases like, "I know you may think I'm just doing this because of the appreciation project, but I really do value it when you . . ." After a while, people are aware that everyone in the training is trying new actions in relating to others, and it becomes the norm.

Q. Is there anything else we should know about the "weirdness factor" and what to do about it?

A. Relax and don't worry about it. Go ahead and act—do something to apply the appreciation concepts in your relationships. Practicing the model on a daily basis actually makes the weirdness go away more quickly (it is repetition, not time, that diminishes our fears). Finally, give your colleagues the benefit of the doubt—assume they mean well and are sincere. It takes some courage to communicate appreciation in a work setting where that hasn't been the standard practice. Then tell them "Thanks" for the effort!

www.appreciationatwork.com

Real Men Don't Need Encouragement (False)

Sometimes we hear someone with whom we are working say: "I don't need to be encouraged." "I don't need anyone to tell me 'You're doing a good job.' I encourage myself. Others may need to feel appreciated, but I don't."

But what we have found, when we dig deeper with these independent types (and they are usually men) is that they have a very narrow definition of encouragement or appreciation. What they usually mean is, "Receiving direct verbal praise or compliments from others isn't that important to me" (which may be true). And many people have learned to be more self-motivating rather than looking to others for encouragement and support, which is fine.

But let's frame the issue a bit differently. First, let's acknowledge that work by its nature is difficult, especially over the long haul. Work would be easy if it was just that—doing our job. But the reality is, there are all kinds of challenges and obstacles that make doing our job that much harder. Consider the following list of things that come up during our workdays:

- computer problems
- others not getting their work done on time or correctly
- losing customers to competitors
- payments coming in late
- financial difficulties (funding not coming in, loans not being approved)
- staff problems, employees resigning
- personal/family issues, health problems

- transportation challenges (stuck in traffic, air travel delays)

- mail or email getting lost

- the copier or printer not working

- running out of materials needed to do the job

- important meetings being delayed

- changes mandated by the organization's leadership

- economic difficulties that negatively impact sales or funding

- changes in governmental rules and regulations that create more work

All of us experience one or more of these challenges every week. And that is what wears on us and makes work hard.

Now, even though there are individuals who don't need much verbal affirmation, if we also take away all the various kinds of rewards that are intrinsic in doing our work, the reality becomes evident. We all need encouragement to keep going—it just comes in different forms. Consider the following benefits we may experience from doing our work:

- a personal sense of well-being when completing a task

- repeat business or referrals to new customers

- growth in our skills and experience

- learning how to do tasks better (sometimes through mistakes we make)

- financial compensation (payment for goods and services)

- realizing a profit

- appreciation from customers and clients

- compliments from others (colleagues, vendors, customers, competitors, business friends)

- suggestions for new and improved goods or services you could provide

- creating a positive reputation in the community

- acknowledgments by your peers (professional organizations, trade associations, awards from civic organizations)

- publicity in local or regional media (newspaper, business publications, television)

- ability to grow your business/organization to serve more people

- quality products and/or high-level services provided

- others calling you to set up appointments to spend time with you (lunch, business meetings)

- verbal comments and compliments from those with whom you work

So, here's the reality check. Take the circumstances from the first list, take away all of the positive rewards from the second list, and honestly tell yourself that, over a long period of time, you wouldn't become worn down and eventually, discouraged. Work takes time, mental and physical energy, and emotional effort. Without some positive feedback, we become burned out.

We all need encouragement—just in different ways. So don't allow yourself to be hoodwinked or misled by the tough guy who says, "Real men don't need encouragement." He just may not need to hear it verbally as much as others do. But find out what his true language is. At some point, he will need some encouragement too.

www.appreciationatwork.com

How to Reward Your Employees without Spending a Chunk of Change

One of the biggest issues businesses, and organizations of any type, have to deal with today is the lack of financial resources. We are in a new world where profits are slim in the for-profit sector, contributions are down in the nonprofit sector, and budgets are being reduced in the governmental sector. Virtually every organization has to do more with less. This is creating a tremendous amount of stress within organizations—both for managers and supervisors, as well as for frontline employees and even volunteers. Fewer resources are available for raises, bonuses, perks that were common in the past (use of a company car, tickets to sporting events), and even company parties.

At the same time, team members are dealing with the loss of staff within their departments, so workloads have increased. But budgets for training or technical upgrades have been trimmed. Resources are tight all over. More demands plus fewer resources becomes a perfect recipe for stress. And stress over the long haul leads to burnout and discouragement.

COMMUNICATING MEANINGFUL APPRECIATION

Here is what research shows are effective ways to communicate appreciation and encouragement to your team members, *without having to spend a lot of money*:

1. **Make sure your communication is personal and fitted to the individual.** The key to effective appreciation and encouragement is the sense by the recipient that you mean what you say and that you took time to think about them personally. Conversely,

we have found that a global "Thanks for a job well done" email to a wide range of people across the organization actually generates a negative response from most team members, given its impersonal nature and perceived minimal effort to complete.

2. **"Speak the language" of the person you are trying to encourage.** If the action we take to communicate appreciation to our colleagues isn't what is important to them, we have wasted our time and effort. This is why we developed the **MBA Inventory**—to identify each team member's preferred languages of appreciation and to specify the actions most valued by them.

3. **The languages of appreciation people value the most don't have to cost a lot of money.** Sure, almost everyone would like a bonus or a raise, but for most organizations that is not possible. To recap, the ways that people experience appreciation in the workplace fall into five categories:

- **Words of Affirmation**
- **Quality Time**
- **Acts of Service**
- **Tangible Gifts**
- **Appropriate Physical Touch**

Most of these don't cost anything financially (even tangible gifts don't have to cost much). Examples include:

- A note from your supervisor complimenting you on the good job you're doing.
- A team member stopping by your office for a few minutes just to catch up.

- A colleague noticing you're "buried" and helping out.

- A gift card you receive as a reward for completing a big project.

- A round of high fives from coworkers after you finish an important presentation.

None of these cost much money. But the key is to be able to use the right action with the right person, at the right time, and with a genuine spirit of appreciation. Then your actions will "hit the target" and be effective in encouraging those with whom you work.

www.appreciationatwork.com

Top Ten Easiest Ways to Express Appreciation to Almost Anyone

1. **Give a verbal compliment** (say, "Thanks for . . ."; tell them, "I'm glad you are part of the team").

2. **Write an email** ("I just wanted to let you know . . ."; "It is really helpful to me when you . . .").

3. **Stop by and see how your colleague is doing.** Spend a few minutes just chatting and checking in on them.

4. **Do something with your coworkers**, like eating together.

5. **Do a small task for someone spontaneously** (hold open the door, offer to carry something).

6. **Stop by their workspace and see if they need any help getting something done.**

7. **Buy them coffee, a drink, a snack, or dessert.**

8. **Get them a magazine related to an area of interest they have** (sports, hobbies, a place they would like to visit).

9. **Give them a high five when they have completed a task** (especially one that has been challenging or that they have been working on awhile).

10. **Greet your colleague warmly.** Say something like, "It's good to see you!" or "How is your day going?"

www.appreciationatwork.com

Empower your workplace
by encouraging people.

appreciationatwork.com

- ✓ Increase loyalty with employees and volunteers
- ✓ Show physical touch appropriately

- ✓ Improve your ability to show appreciation
- ✓ Reduce cynicism and create a positive environment

The 5 Languages of Appreciation

curriculum

For more information on the curriculum visit

appreciationatwork.com

NORTHFIELD
PUBLISHING

northfieldpublishing.com

THE FIVE LANGUAGES OF APOLOGY

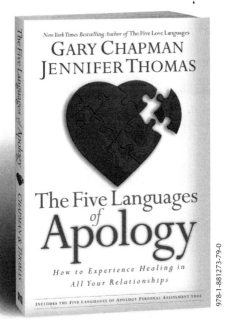

Just as you have a distinct love language, you also hear and express the words and gestures of apology in a different language. This groundbreaking study of the way we apologize reveals that it's not a matter of will—it's a matter of how. By helping you identify the languages of apology, this book clears the way toward healing and sustaining vital relationships.

northfieldpublishing.com